Specia
Schoo..

T is book provides a concise but comprehensive overview of key
ues in provision for children with special educational needs in
ools, emphasizing the role of the mainstream class teacher.

numerous changes in special educational policy and practice
have taken place since the first edition was published are dealt
h in this second edition. It incorporates discussion of current
ates concerning the nature of special educational needs and of
usive educational practice. It brings the discussion of legislative
policy frameworks up to date and highlights the importance of
active involvement of the children themselves in the educational
cesses of assessment, planning and review.

ial Educational Needs in Schools opens with an exploration of
ent concepts of special educational need and a detailed consid-
ion of the legislation and policies which underpin special
cational provision. It goes on to examine significant principles
rriculum development, and presents an evaluation of methods
sessment and teaching strategies for meeting children's needs.
book concludes with a discussion of the sources of support that
pen to teachers to help them meet the necessary standards.

lly **Beveridge** is Senior Lecturer in Education at the University of
ds.

Special Educational Needs in Schools

Second edition

Sally Beveridge

London and New York

First published 1993
Reprinted 1995

Second edition first published 1999
by Routledge
11 New Fetter Lane, London EC4P 4EE

Simultaneously published in the USA and Canada
by Routledge
29 West 35th Street, New York, NY 10001

Reprinted 2001 by RoutledgeFalmer

RoutledgeFalmer is an imprint of the Taylor & Francis Group

Typeset in Palatino by Routledge
Printed and bound in Great Britain by
TJ International, Padstow, Cornwall

British Library Cataloguing in Publication Data
A catalogue record for this book is available from the British
Library

Library of Congress Cataloging in Publication Data
Beveridge, Sally
Special educational needs in schools / Sally Beveridge – 2nd ed.
p. cm.
Includes bibliographical references and index.
1. Special education–Great Britain. 2. Mainstreaming in
education–Great Britain. 3. Education and state–Great Britain.
I. Title.
LC3986.G7B48   1999
371.9'0941–dc 21   99-13192
CIP

ISBN 0415–20293–0 (hbk)
ISBN 0415–20294–9 (pbk)

Contents

Figures

Acknowledgements

I am grateful to Susan Cain, Stuart Hemingway and Phil Jackson for allowing me to use their examples of school policy and assessment practice. My thanks also go to Patrick Wiegand for his constructive comments on the preparation of this second edition of the book.

Chapter 1

Concepts of special educational need

All children can be regarded as having special needs of some kind during their school careers, and there are few of us who, when looking back at our own time as pupils, cannot recollect particular instances where we experienced difficulties in learning or in social contexts. This does not imply, however, that we were necessarily judged by our teachers to be in need of special educational help. For this to have happened, we would have to have been among a minority of pupils whose difficulties were assessed as significantly different from those of their peers. The criteria for such an assessment, and the resulting proportions of pupils who are so identified, have fluctuated over time, for the concept of special educational need is socially constructed. As such, it changes over time in a way which is influenced both by prevalent expectations about children's educational progress and also by political and economic concerns.

The present concept of special educational need is based on the deliberations of the Warnock Committee, which had a governmental brief to investigate and make recommendations about special educational provision, and which published its report in 1978 (DES 1978). The Committee brought together and articulated the views that were current among many of those who were working in special education, and it was generally held to represent a major development in official thinking about special educational need. Although not all of its recommendations were adopted, it has been of lasting significance, not least because of its insistence that special educational need and special educational provision are central concerns for all who are involved in education, rather than subjects for specialist interest only.

Background to the Warnock recommendations

Prior to the publication of the Warnock Report, models of special educational need which emphasized deficits within the child from a medical or psychological perspective were predominant. The need for special educational 'treatment' was associated with the notion of 'disability of mind or body'. The 1944 Education Act had defined eleven categories of disability. These excluded a group of children who were deemed 'ineducable' on account of the severity of their 'handicaps', but included varying degrees of blindness or deafness, physical impairment, speech defects, educational 'subnormality' and 'maladjustment'. It may be noted that, apart from the latter two categories, disabilities were described in medical terms and their diagnosis appeared to be relatively clear-cut. Educational subnormality and maladjustment were more difficult to determine, implying as they did some value judgements about the cut-off point between 'normal' and 'abnormal' levels of individual variation in learning and in social and emotional development. As these were to become by far the largest of the categories described in the legislation, concerns were increasingly raised about the appropriateness of their definition, particularly as it was found that diagnosis seemed to be associated with certain ethnic and social class variables. Concerns were also voiced that, no matter how severe their impairments, no children should be regarded as ineducable. This argument gathered considerable support, and in 1970 legislation was introduced whereby LEAs were required to make special educational provision for all types of disability. Although it was not stipulated that this provision should necessarily take the form of separate schools or classes, this became the predominant practice and, as a result, 'special education' tended to be regarded as that which occurred in special schools.

Warnock's approach

The Warnock Committee took a much wider view of special education. Drawing attention to the significant numbers of children in ordinary schools who at some time experience difficulties in their learning, it argued that it was not helpful to think in terms of a dichotomy between their educational needs and those of the pupils in special schools. Rather, it wished to see an acknowledgement of the continuum of individual educational need among all pupils. From this broader perspective, special education could be defined as 'any form of additional help, wherever it is provided ... to overcome educational difficulty' (DES 1978: para. 1.10).

In extending the scope of special education in this way, the Warnock Committee was not suggesting that large numbers of children in ordinary schools should be regarded as having disabilities. On the contrary, it recommended that the existing categorization of disability was educationally inappropriate and should be abolished. It pointed out that to categorize children in such a way could be stigmatizing and, further, that to describe a child as having a particular disability was of little help when it came to determining what sort of educational provision might best meet the child's needs. Children quite frequently have more than one form of difficulty, and that which is most significant from a medical point of view is not necessarily of the greatest educational relevance. Further, there is wide individual variation between the educational needs of children who have the same form of disability, and an undue focus on their impairment can distract attention from other important influences on their learning. The Committee proposed, therefore, that instead of the previous categories a generic term of 'learning difficulties' should be applied to embrace all those pupils who, for whatever reasons, require additional educational help. Figure 1.1 shows three dimensions of learning difficulty that are described in the Warnock Report. From this it can be seen that special educational needs might be long-lasting or short-term, specific to particular aspects of learning or more general, and will also vary in the degree to which they affect a child's learning. In recognition of this variation, the Warnock Committee suggested that learning difficulties could be further described as 'mild', 'moderate', 'severe' or 'specific'.

It has frequently been noted that by making this suggestion, rather than abolishing categorization, the Committee effectively provided the basis for a new method of categorizing educational needs. While this has indeed proved to be the case, it does not detract from the importance of the Committee's arguments for a shift away from psychological–medical models of children's

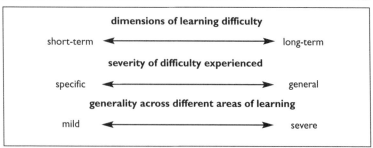

Figure 1.1   Dimensions of learning difficulty in Warnock's continuum of special educational need

learning difficulties. Its line of reasoning represents an explicit attempt to break with traditional notions of educational difficulty as being primarily rooted and fixed within the individual child. It did not deny that within-child factors can have a significant impact on learning, but the concept of special educational need which was put forward was far more concerned with the interaction between the child and the learning contexts which the child experiences. An interactive explanation of educational need has, as the Committee argued, many more positive implications for schools than are offered by traditional models. It allows us to view children's needs as a result of a mismatch between the knowledge, skills and experiences they bring to their learning situations and the demands that are made of them. From this perspective, there are constructive steps that can be taken to overcome or even prevent learning difficulties.

The principle that children's special educational needs cannot be viewed in isolation from the learning contexts in which they arise is further emphasized by the three aspects of need that are identified in the Warnock Report:

(i)   the provision of special means of access to the curriculum;
(ii) the provision of a special or modified curriculum;
(iii) particular attention to the social structure and emotional climate in which education takes place.

(DES 1978: para. 3.19)

The first of these provisions is not controversial. Where children have difficulties which prevent them from gaining access to the curriculum in the usual way, then clearly they need whatever help is necessary to allow them to participate as fully as possible in the learning experiences that are provided. For example, children with sensory or physical impairments may need special equipment or attention to positioning, and others will benefit from the use of adapted written material. The second and third provisions have given rise to rather more debate, however. Though not denying that the curriculum and the social and emotional climate are important influences on children's learning, some (e.g. Galloway 1985) have suggested that children may too readily be transferred to different curricular activities and social groupings, and that there is no guarantee that this will help them overcome their difficulties. They point out that the 'ordinary' curriculum and climate for learning in schools can add to as well as alleviate children's difficulties, and argue that the better these are matched to the needs of all pupils, then the less likelihood there will be that substantial numbers of children will be regarded as having needs which require special educational provision.

The fact that there is considerable variation between schools in the proportion of their pupils who experience educational difficulties is not in doubt. Indeed, an acceptance of the interactive nature of special educational needs implies an acknowledgement of their relativity. Thus, a child who is identified as having learning difficulties in one school would not automatically be judged in the same way in another. The child's needs, therefore, can be seen to be relative to those of the other pupils in the school, the teachers' knowledge, skills and approach, the school's approach to individual diversity, LEA policy, and so on. Given this relativity, it is not surprising to find that estimates of the prevalence of special educational needs are problematic. On the basis of the research evidence that was available to them, the Warnock Committee estimated that as many as 20 per cent of pupils might have such needs at some point in their school career and, although certain reservations have been voiced, this figure has until now been generally accepted.

The implications of the Warnock Committee's approach

In summing up the Warnock Committee's approach to the concept of special educational needs, it would be fair to say that it was representative of the opinions of many of those who were involved in special education at the time. Among these professionals, there was a large degree of acceptance of the notion that the scope of special education should be conceived much more broadly, and that a continuum of special educational needs, with particular attention to their interactive and relative nature, should be recognized. The new concept did, though, have wide-ranging and major implications for ordinary schools and their teachers. Previously, it had been possible to see special education as separate from the ordinary school system. Where significant learning difficulties were experienced by pupils in ordinary classes, there were channels for referring these pupils for special help elsewhere. If one in five pupils were to be regarded as having such difficulties, however, then it became apparent that special education must be conceived as an integral part of the whole educational system. Fewer than 2 per cent of pupils had traditionally been educated in separate special provision and therefore the vast majority of pupils with special educational needs had always been educated in ordinary schools. It followed therefore that all teachers must be seen to have a responsibility for making special educational provision for those pupils experiencing learning difficulties in their classes. Furthermore, the acknowledgement of the interactive and relative nature of those pupils' needs made it clear that both teachers individually and schools collectively have a significant role to play in alleviating or adding to their difficulties. In order to explore the nature of that role, it is necessary to look more closely at the implications of the main features of the Warnock Committee's concept of special educational need.

The interactive nature of special educational need

Most teachers accept, at least in principle, that the educational difficulties which children experience can only be fully understood by reference to the contexts in which they arise. Although it is clear that some children have cognitive limitations or other impairments that impede their progress, it is also generally acknowledged that there can be very different educational outcomes for such children. Among the complex and interacting factors that contribute to this diversity, the attitudes and expectations of others, and the type of support, knowledge and understanding that they experience at home, at school and in their local community, all play a significant part.

Few teachers need persuading of the importance of home background factors in children's attainment and behaviour at school. For most children home is clearly not only their first and primary learning environment, but one which continues to exert a powerful influence. Further, there is ample research evidence to demonstrate an association between poor educational achievement and measures of social disadvantage (Sammons and Mortimore 1990), although it should be noted that there are a number of different explanations put forward for this finding. Teachers frequently cite parental attitudes to school and apparent interest in their children's education as critical factors, and there is no doubt that good home–school relationships can have an essential role in children's learning. In order to foster such relations, however, positive attitudes towards and interest in parental perspectives on the part of schools are likely to be as important as home background variables.

It is particularly important that the acknowledgement of the significant influence of home on attainment at school should not lead to the conclusion that schools themselves have only a subsidiary role to play. On the contrary; the evidence from research into school effectiveness at both primary and secondary levels (Rutter *et al.* 1979; Mortimore *et al.* 1988) is that schools vary in their effectiveness in educating pupils even when they come from similar home backgrounds and have similar initial levels of achievement. A recognition of the impact that schools can have on the difficulties experienced by some of their pupils may not be widespread among teachers, however. For example, in a study of special educational needs in junior schools, Croll and Moses (1985) asked teachers for their explanation of the needs of children in their classes. The vast majority of references were to 'within-child' factors for those with learning difficulties, and to home background for those with emotional or behavioural difficulties. Mention of school-based factors was made in fewer than 4 per cent of all cases. Many changes have been introduced in schools since this study took place. Nevertheless, researchers (e.g. Ainscow 1995a; Clark *et al.* 1997) continue to report the lasting influence among teachers of similar perspectives which, with their emphasis on individual child and/or family deficits, can distract attention from school-based strategies for overcoming special educational needs.

The scope of special educational needs

In their survey of junior schools Croll and Moses (1985) found that, on average, class teachers judged 18.8 per cent of their pupils to have some form of special educational need. As under 2 per cent of pupils were placed in special schools at the time, this might be taken as strong support for Warnock's estimate. However, it has been argued that the figure of 20 per cent has become a target (e.g. Ainscow and Muncey 1989) and that given the expectation that there will be this proportion of pupils experiencing difficulties, schools are likely to identify and categorize a group of their lowest achieving pupils accordingly. This is perhaps a rather over-simplified interpretation, as all the evidence suggests considerable variation between schools in the numbers of pupils judged to have special educational needs. Nevertheless, government statistics for 1997 reveal that across the country schools continue to identify approximately 18 per cent of their pupils as having such needs (DfEE 1997a), and concerns have been voiced that a fixed notion of a distinct group of this size has become established (e.g. Thomas 1995; Davie 1996). The identification of need may often be more influenced by the local and national educational criteria currently in use than by an individual pupil's characteristics, and for this reason not all have welcomed the way in which the scope of special education has been broadened since the publication of the Warnock Report. Their concerns focus both on which children are identified as in need, and also on what follows from their identification.

Sociologists of education such as Tomlinson (1981, 1982) have in the past drawn attention to the disproportionate representation of 'relatively powerless groups in society' in those special schools that cater for pupils with moderate learning difficulties and emotional and behavioural difficulties. Tomlinson has argued that factors of socio-economic and ethnic status are significantly associated with the identification of these forms of special educational need, and that as the scope of special education expands within ordinary schools so larger and larger numbers of children from the lowest status families will be judged to have such difficulties.

Most of those concerned with special education would accept the evidence that social factors are involved in the identification of special educational need. Indeed, the influence of gender, as well as of socio-economic class and ethnicity, has frequently been documented. There is rather more debate, however, about the impact of identification on the pupils concerned. The Warnock Committee made it quite clear that it saw identification as a positive first step for any pupil who was experiencing difficulties. It recommended that all schools should have procedures which enable them to identify pupils as early as possible, so that special help can be given both to enable pupils to overcome their current difficulties and, hopefully, to prevent more serious difficulties from arising subsequently. By contrast, Tomlinson, while not denying the importance of such 'humanitarian' motives for the identification of special educational need, argues that historically it has often served a different purpose. She suggests that, rather than being primarily concerned with the needs of individuals, special education has traditionally acted as a 'safety valve' for the ordinary education system, by removing those pupils who posed a challenge to its smooth operation. As a result, an extensive specialist and separate service has grown up with a focus on individual difficulties, and this has served to distract attention from what might be problematic in the ordinary school system. Furthermore, whether pupils have been removed to different groups in ordinary schools or to special schools, they have typically been provided with different curricular experiences. Tomlinson concludes that these are of lower status than the experiences of their peers, and that this, in conjunction with lowered expectations of the pupils, is likely to lead to the poor progress that is taken to justify the initial assessment of educational difficulty. Thus, given that most of the pupils come from low-status families, she characterizes special education as a form of 'social control'.

Not surprisingly, Tomlinson's position has proved to be

controversial. Cole (1989), for example, maintains that her historical perspective is selective. Although he accepts that the social control hypothesis has some substance, he puts forward an alternative analysis which leads him to conclude that humanitarian motives have been far more influential in the development of special education than Tomlinson implies. Nevertheless, a major theme emerges from her arguments which remains particularly significant in continuing debates. This is the principle that the needs of individual children cannot be viewed in isolation from the wider social context in which they occur. At the level of society, Barton (1995) and Dyson (1997) are among those who argue that current concepts of special educational need must be 'reconnected' with the political issues of rights and power that are associated with disadvantage and inequality. At the school level, it has been argued that children who are experiencing learning or emotional and behavioural difficulties can show up weaknesses in the school's curriculum. This is a perspective associated with a model which Clark and her colleagues (Clark *et al.* 1995) characterize as organizational, and can be illustrated by Galloway's observation:

> The question is whether a curriculum and emotional climate which fails to cater for up to 20 per cent of pupils can be entirely suitable for the remaining 80 per cent.
>
> (Galloway 1985: 6)

From this point of view, special educational needs are seen to arise as a result of aspects of the organization and curriculum in school. Rather than seeking within-child reasons for the difficulties that children experience, therefore, the task is to seek changes to those aspects of school practice which would make them more responsive to pupil diversity. Drawing on principles derived from school effectiveness research, a significant element of school which is frequently highlighted concerns teacher expectations. It is significant therefore that raising expectations is described by the current government as a 'key principle' underpinning a range of initiatives which aim to raise the standards achieved by children with special educational needs and, in so doing, to reduce the proportions who are identified as having such needs (DfEE 1998a).

The continuum of educational need

The notion of a continuum of educational need was fundamental to the Warnock Committee's thinking. The traditional view of discrete categories of pupils, made up of those who require special educational help and those who do not, served not only to emphasize differences rather than similarities between children, but also to distract attention from the diversity of individual need that all can experience in their learning. Among teachers, the recognition of such diversity may be reflected in the scepticism some demonstrate when they refer to the 'myth of the normal child', or in the more frequently expressed view that 'all children are special'. On the whole this does not, of course, prevent them from making relative judgements about children in which general expectations about 'normal' progress are implicit. Thus, for example, a pupil's attainment may be described as 'above' or 'below' average, and behaviour may be judged to be 'mature' or 'immature'. Those pupils whose attainment and behaviour are significantly poorer than those of their peers will rightly cause their teachers concern. However, what becomes problematic when considering the continuum of children's needs is the question of at what point do individual educational needs become 'special'?

Any cut-off point on a continuum can seem arbitrary and this, coupled with the recognition of the relativity of needs, has led to some uncertainty in decisions about what constitutes special educational need. There are those who think that we should abandon the term altogether. It seems apparent that, when applied as a label to children, it can lead to as much stigmatization, devaluing and negative emphasis on difference as the former categories of disability that the Warnock Committee sought to replace. For this reason, there are those (e.g. Hart 1996) who argue that it is more appropriate to refer only to 'individual educational needs'. Some (e.g. Booth 1998) also dislike the way the term directs attention to a child 'having' special educational needs, thus appearing to locate the problem with the individual child. They argue that the focus should be redirected onto barriers to children's learning. By contrast, others (e.g. Roaf and Bines 1989) see the concept of special educational need as fundamentally linked to principles of equal opportunities and rights. Children who experience difficulties in their learning may often be afforded low status in schools, particularly when accountability is measured primarily by academic achievement, and this status is likely to affect decisions about resource alloca- tion. Yet these children need additional help if they are to make the most of their educational opportunities. If the necessary resources for this assistance are to be made available, then it seems clear that relevant differences must be identified and acknowl- edged. As Roaf points out, 'To ignore differences altogether, or to pay too much attention to irrelevant differences, are both equally unjust' (1989: 93).

From this perspective, what becomes crucial is not the label 'special educational need' itself, but a clarification of its distinction from other forms of educational need. Norwich (1996), for example, puts forward a framework for distinguishing between: common learning needs, shared with all a child's peers; individual needs, which reflect the range of individual diversity; and exceptional needs, which arise from special characteristics or circumstances and which may be shared with a subgroup of peers. Exceptional needs include aspects of children's learning, emotional and behavioural difficulties, but go beyond current definitions of special educational need. There has been increasing recognition of the common princi- ples that underpin aspects of provision for children with special educational needs and for those learning English as a second language, those who are exceptionally able, those whose needs arise from disrupted schooling, and so on (e.g. Davie 1996). Norwich's categorization represents one attempt to incorporate the whole range of exceptional needs within a unifying framework.

This approach does not deny the possibility of stigma: it is only too apparent that any label which is applied to a minority group can acquire derogatory overtones. Unfortunately, however, this may happen with or without the use of officially recognized terminology. Rather than seeking to abandon the label of special educational need, therefore, it may be a more effective strategy to tackle ques- tions of stigma by giving explicit recognition and value to individual difference and by celebrating diversity. The potential impact of such a strategy can be illustrated, for example, by the pride which many deaf people take in their deaf identity. What is clear is that, in addition to responding to the needs and rights of children with special educational needs, the educational task must also address the promotion of positive attitudes, values and behaviour among their peers.

How special are special educational needs?

Current approaches to conceptualizing special educational need, with their emphasis on its relative and interactive nature, are complex and multi-faceted. Although the Warnock Report signalled a move away from simple psychological–medical explanations, debates continue on the relative importance of such factors, the ways in which these interact with curriculum and organizational arrangements, and the impact of the social and political context (see, for example, Clark *et al*. 1998).

There has been a growing concern that the current definition of special educational need requires clarification in order to distinguish its overlaps and boundaries with other forms of educational need. While the government has acknowledged that the term is open to differing interpretations, it has no immediate plans to review the legal definition (DfEE 1998a). However, the question of just how far special educational needs should be regarded as special is an important one for teachers because not only are they the people who in most cases will identify these needs, but they also have a responsibility for meeting them (DfE 1994a). Teachers vary in their willingness to make an early decision that the difficulties an individual pupil is experiencing are significant enough to describe as special. They are influenced in this by the sorts of argument that have been discussed in this chapter, as well as by their feelings of professional competence in responding to diverse individual needs. They are also guided by school and LEA policies which determine the nature and extent of additional resources to meet identified needs. In practice, they are likely to identify as having special educational needs those children whom they find most difficult to teach because of poor progress and achievement or problematic behaviour, or both.

There is no doubt that children with learning and emotional or behavioural difficulties pose a challenge to teachers. However, the extent of their needs must be seen as relative to the quality of the educational experiences with which they are provided. It has often been argued that what is needed by children with special educational needs is good overall educational practice, and there is some evidence to support such a view. The HMI survey of special educational needs in ordinary schools (1989), for example, concluded that the 'features of good practice' that it was able to identify 'applied to the teaching of all pupils, and not just to those with special educational need' (ibid.: para. 26). This perspective has led some researchers to argue that it is by making schools more effective for all children that one improves special educational provision. For example, Ainscow and his colleagues (Ainscow 1995b) have sought ways of applying general principles derived from school effectiveness research in order to help schools restructure their provision to meet special educational needs. By contrast, Reynolds (1995) has cautioned that schools can be differentially effective: for example, the introduction of changes intended to benefit one group of pupils may not necessarily help others; and, furthermore, particular approaches directed towards enhancing academic achievement may have less positive effects on social outcomes. Nevertheless, a school's responsiveness to special educational needs cannot be readily separated out from its overall responsiveness to pupil diversity.

The acceptance of a continuum of educational need implies that a continuum may also be described in the sort of educational help that children require. From this perspective, special education is not regarded as necessarily being qualitatively different from other education, but rather as different in the degree of assistance and support that may be given. This is neither to deny nor to undervalue the specific expertise of those teachers who work with pupils with severe and specialist needs. It does emphasize, however, that all teachers need to develop their practice and their responsiveness to individual differences in ways which can help children overcome their educational difficulties.

Discussion points

1 'All children are special.' What arguments can be made for and against the proposition that we should move towards a concept of 'individual' rather than 'special' educational needs?

2 'The fact that a child has special needs does not necessarily imply that the child, as an individual, needs help. The most

effective way to help the child may be to review aspects of school organisation, or teaching methods and resources' (Galloway 1985). How far does the recognition that special educational needs are both relative and interactive in nature lend support to this perspective?

3 Tomlinson characterizes special educational provision as a form of 'social control'. What concerns do her arguments raise for teachers, and how far are these justified?

Further reading

Ainscow, M. (ed.) (1991) *Effective Schools for All*, London: David Fulton.

Clark, C., Dyson, A. and Millward, A. (eds) (1998) *Theorising Special Education*, London: Routledge.

Chapter 2

The legislative framework

Background: the 1981 Education Act

The influence of the Warnock Report (DES 1978) was not restricted to a new conceptualization of special educational needs; it also made wide-ranging recommendations about the way in which special educational provision should be developed. The Committee argued that this provision should be seen as 'additional or supplementary' rather than 'separate or alternative' to regular education, and described a continuum of settings in which it might take place. For most children, their needs would be met in ordinary classrooms, with additional support as required. In order that their rights to special educational provision were safeguarded, a system for identifying and assessing needs was proposed and, where these could not be met within ordinary school resources, LEAs should draw on the advice of a wide range of professionals in order to determine the appropriate form of additional help. Importantly, parents were to be seen as key participants in the decision-making process. Indeed, a central theme of the Warnock Report was that a partnership between schools and parents was crucial to the children's successful education. Many of the Warnock Committee's recommendations were taken up in the 1981 Education Act. The main provisions of this Act were concerned with definitions of special educational need and provision, the role of ordinary schools in meeting special educational needs, the identification and assessment of need and the rights of parents in the decision-making process. Although the 1981 Act itself has now been replaced by more recent legislation, its main provisions continue to underpin the statutory framework for special education, and it is therefore appropriate to outline them briefly here.

Definitions of special educational need and provision

The previous statutory categories of disability were replaced in the 1981 Act by one of special educational need. The definition of special educational need, as a number of commentators have pointed out, is somewhat circular. That is, a child is to be regarded as having special educational needs if he or she has 'a learning difficulty which calls for special educational provision to be made'. While no further criteria are provided to determine exactly what constitutes this level of difficulty, reference is made to children whose difficulties are 'significantly greater' than those experienced by others of the same age, as well as to those with a disability that impedes access to the facilities which are generally provided. Children of below school age, who are thought likely to fall into one of these categories later if they do not receive special pre-school help, are also included in the definition. However, those whose educational difficulties are solely related to the fact that the language used at school is different from that used at home are specifically excluded. Special educational provision was described as 'additional to, or otherwise different from' that which is generally made for pupils.

The role of ordinary schools

LEAs were required by the 1981 Act to ensure that children with special educational needs were educated in ordinary schools, provided certain conditions were met. The conditions, which allowed for a considerable range of interpretation, were that the views of the child's parents must be taken into account, and that placement in an ordinary school must be compatible not only with the child receiving the special provision required, but also with the effective education of the other pupils there and with the efficient use of resources. It was stipulated that where children are educated in ordinary schools, then they should be involved 'in the activities of the school together with children who do not have special educational needs' (Section 2 (7)). Both LEAs and school governors were charged with responsibilities to keep the arrangements made for meeting special educational needs under review.

Identification and assessment procedures

The Act made it clear that ordinary schools had a responsibility to identify, assess and provide for the majority of children with special educational needs and to monitor their progress. It did not specify what form school-based assessment should take. It did, however, outline in great detail the procedures for formal statutory assessments which should be undertaken by the LEA for the minority of children whose special educational needs were such that they could not be met within 'generally available resources'. In these cases, the LEA was to initiate multiprofessional assessment and to invite parents to contribute their advice, in order to inform a decision about whether or not a statement of special educational need was required. If a statement was drawn up, this must specify, first, the precise nature of the child's assessed difficulties and educational needs, and, second, the special or additional provision that would be made in order to meet the child's needs. The statement must then be reviewed at least annually, with a reassessment, usually at the age of about 13½ years.

Parental involvement in the decision-making process

Parental rights in relation to the statutory assessment procedures were also specified in detail. Parents were to be informed and consulted at all stages and, in the event of unresolved disagreements with the LEA, had a right of appeal to an Appeals Committee and, beyond that, to the Secretary of State.

The implementation of the 1981 Education Act

Those working in special education greeted the 1981 Education Act with some ambivalence. Most welcomed the way in which it set special education within the mainstream of educational thinking and emphasized the scope and relativity of special educational needs. Reaction to its clauses concerning placement in ordinary schools was more mixed: the emphasis on where children were placed rather than the quality of their education caused concern. At the same time, the Act was also disappointing to those who had hoped for a less equivocal stance on the issue of inclusion. While a duty was placed on LEAs to make special educational provision in ordinary schools, the provisos that were attached to this were sufficient to allow them to maintain their previous approach towards the placement of pupils in separate schools or classes. Indeed, a comparative study of LEA practice in the years following its implementation (Swann 1988a) revealed that whereas some authorities were placing proportionally more children with special educational needs in ordinary schools, others were increasing their provision in separate schools and classes.

The formal statementing procedures that were introduced also provoked a great deal of debate. These were designed to safeguard additional resources for those children with the most evident needs, but Dessent (1987) was among those who argued that they run contrary to the principle of a continuum of need. That is, the focus that they place on a particular minority serves to distract attention from others with special educational needs, and thereby perpetuates traditional notions of categorization. There were also a number of practical difficulties in implementing the procedures. Goacher and his colleagues (1988) found clear evidence of considerable variability between LEAs both in the criteria they employed in their assessment of need and therefore in the proportions of pupils with statements, and also in the extent of the additional resources that they provided. Furthermore, they found that statements were frequently written in general and non-specific terms, and anxieties were raised that, in a time of financial constraint, the special provision that was outlined on a statement might be influenced as much by resource implications as by the assessment of individual need. Finally, while in principle the process of consultation with parents and with all professionals concerned was generally welcomed, the time-consuming and bureaucratic nature of the procedures, even when there was total agreement about a child's need for additional help, was widely criticized.

In principle, the Act extended parental rights to participate in educational decision-making, at least where their children's needs were judged to be sufficiently significant to warrant formal assessment. However, it did not take up the Warnock Committee's recommendation that parents should be allocated a 'named person' who could offer advice and support. In the absence of such assistance, it was not at all clear how parents would be sufficiently informed to exercise their rights. Research evidence quickly accumulated (e.g. Sandow *et al.* 1987; Vaughan 1989) that neither in the initial assessment nor subsequently did parents perceive themselves as 'equal partners' with the professionals involved, and few felt that they had been able to make a significant contribution to the decision-making process.

There were, then, a number of practical problems in the implementation of the 1981 Education Act. However, it is important to emphasize that, at the same time, it led to several very positive changes. First, there is no doubt that it served to raise general awareness about the range of special educational needs that children may experience, and to place these needs firmly in the context of mainstream educational practice. Second, within mainstream schools, a change began to be seen in the role and status of staff who were designated as having a particular responsibility for pupils with special educational needs. These staff, who had often formerly been referred to as 'remedial teachers', traditionally spent most of their time working directly with pupils in separate classes and groups. Frequently they, like the pupils they taught, were reported to hold low status in the school, and the work they did was often somewhat detached from that of their colleagues. However, increasingly some of them began to take on a more extensive and central role, frequently characterized as that of 'special needs coordinator'. That is, in addition to their direct teaching duties they were also given responsibilities to coordinate and monitor the learning experiences provided for pupils with special educational needs throughout the school. These changes were associated with the gradual emergence of what has become known as a 'whole school approach', in which special educational provision is recognized as an integral part of the work of a school and all teachers are explicitly regarded as teachers of pupils with special educational needs.

The progress that had been made since the Act was introduced as well as the continuing areas for concern were summarized by the House of Commons Select Committee which met in 1987 to review its implementation. This Committee acknowledged that there was still some confusion about the concept of special educational need and that its relativity led to difficulties in decision-making, but overall it reported that the main principles upon which the Act was based had been accepted. It found that special educational provision had become far more integral to the work of ordinary schools than was previously the case, and it gave its full support to the principle of inclusion. While it felt that a great deal had been achieved, it also raised criticisms about the inadequacy of the information and help that was given to parents, and drew attention to the need for clearer guidelines and more streamlined procedures for the drawing up of statements. Importantly, it highlighted the need for a commitment to extra resources if the principles of the Act were to be put fully into practice.

In the same year that the Select Committee presented these findings, however, the Secretary of State for Education introduced detailed and wide-ranging proposals for educational reform which led to considerable apprehension that much of the work of the 1981 Act might be undone. Rather than being integral to the thinking of this 1987 Education Reform Bill, special educational needs were conspicuous by their absence. One reference was made to special schools, and in a further clause it was suggested that children with statements would be exempt from the provisions of the proposed National Curriculum. No mention at all was made of the majority of pupils with special educational needs. The overwhelming response of those involved in special educational provision was that the Bill was incompatible with the principles of the 1981 Act. As a result of extensive lobbying, a number of positive changes were introduced into what became the 1988 Education Reform Act, and these were further reinforced in the circulars of guidance that were issued on its implementation. However, some significant areas for concern remained.

The 1988 Education Reform Act

The 1988 Act introduced a great number of changes to the education system as a whole. Its impact on provision for pupils with special educational needs has been most evident in relation to the National Curriculum and associated programme of assessment, and the devolution of financial management from LEAs to schools.

The National Curriculum

Early fears that a minority of pupils would be automatically exempted from the National Curriculum subsided when the government made it clear that the entitlement to the 'broad and balanced' curriculum that was envisaged applied to all pupils. This was generally welcomed, not only because it was in accordance with principles of equal opportunity, but also because it emphasized a continuum between ordinary and special educational provision. There was some optimism that the entitlement to the National Curriculum might both broaden and raise the status of the learning experiences that were provided for pupils with special educational needs. If it were to do so, however, then it was essential that the full range of individual need should be taken into account in drawing up the curriculum plans and, furthermore, that the implementation of these plans should be sufficiently flexible to allow maximum participation by all pupils.

Initially such flexibility was inhibited by two main factors. First, the specified curriculum content of the National Curriculum was so extensive that it left little time available for the accommodation of children's particular needs. For example, as discussed in Chapter 4, explicit attention to personal and social aspects of education, and opportunities for the repeated consolidation of learning, can be particularly important for children with special educational needs. Second, the demands of the designated programmes of study were tightly tied to Key Stages in ways which could represent a poor match to the needs of children experiencing learning difficulties. However, the revisions to the National Curriculum that were introduced in 1995 have resulted in a greater degree of flexibility on both counts, through a reduction in the amount of specified content and by allowing more freedom for children to work on material appropriate to their levels of achievement.

The 1988 Act provides for two main ways in which the National Curriculum may be formally 'modified' or even 'disapplied'. First, temporary exceptions from the National Curriculum of up to six months, renewable for a further six months, can be sought. These may be used during the time when formal assessment procedures are being carried out which might lead to a statement of special educational need. A more general use is in situations where a pupil's 'circumstances' or 'conduct' are judged such as to make National Curriculum requirements inappropriate. The decision to seek a temporary exception rests largely with the headteacher, although he or she must inform the pupil's parents, as well as the school governors and the LEA, and the parents have a right of appeal. It has always been emphasized that temporary exceptions should only be used very rarely, and this has certainly been the case to date (Friel 1997). Second, when children have statements of special educational need, exceptions can be made to 'any or all' of the requirements of the National Curriculum. In those cases where exceptions are judged appropriate then the statements must be amended to indicate their precise nature, and must further specify the alternative provision that will be substituted in order to maintain a balanced and broadly-based curriculum. Parents must be fully informed of any intended amendment to their child's statement, and have the right of appeal if they disagree with the LEA's decision.

In practice, there has been a general commitment in schools to make the National Curriculum accessible for children with the full range of special educational needs, and formal exceptions from its provisions have been minimal.

National Curriculum assessments

The way in which progress through the National Curriculum is assessed is of particular significance for pupils who experience learning difficulties. Many who are concerned with special educational needs have welcomed the detailed teacher records which form an important part of the National Curriculum assessment process. The continuous curriculum-based assessment forming the core of such records has a potentially valuable role to play not only in alerting teachers to areas of difficulty, but also in planning positive steps to overcome these and in monitoring progress.

The Standard Assessment Tasks (SATs), by contrast, have been greeted with far less enthusiasm. Formalized testing procedures are likely to be particularly stressful for those who lack confidence in themselves as learners, and unless they are sensitively undertaken they may contribute to feelings of failure. Some flexibility in SATs procedures is allowed – for example, in the length of time that is taken, the way in which instructions are given and the form of response that is required – in order to accommodate children with special educational needs. From her review of mainstream practice, Lewis (1996) confirmed that teachers had been able to make skilful adaptations of this kind which facilitated the children's participation. However, questions might be raised about how far such adaptations can be taken and still yield 'standard' assessment information, and it is notable that doubts continue to be aired more generally about the overall reliability of SATs as a measure of attainment. Many would agree with Lewis's conclusion that moderated teacher assessment is 'likely to be fairer to children; more popular with teachers, and possibly parents; and more consistent with the ethos of inclusive schools' (ibid.: 13) than the SATs which have been used to date.

The main focus of concern must be the use to which the results of Standard Assessment Tasks are put. The publication of aggregated results has become a significant means of comparing and judging school performance. This, coupled with the 1988 Act's provisions on open enrolment and the local management of schools, can work to the detriment of those with special educational needs.

Local management of schools

As a result of the Act, by far the largest part of an LEA's budget is devolved to its schools on a formula which is primarily based on the numbers and ages of pupils on roll. Coupled with a policy of open enrolment, this formula effectively acts to put schools in direct competition with one another in order to maintain their pupil numbers. When that competition is based at least in part on the evidence of overall attainments on the National Curriculum, then the presence of a sizeable minority of pupils with learning difficulties can be disadvantageous to a school, and they may be perceived as an unwelcome and unproductive drain on resources. In such circumstances the provision of teaching assistance for these pupils may well be afforded a lower priority (Welton 1989). Furthermore, as their education is relatively expensive, schools may also seek to restrict the numbers of children with special educational needs on their rolls unless they are seen to generate additional resourcing (Lunt 1990).

The introduction of local management of schools made it harder for LEAs to safeguard such resourcing. There is scope for a weighting to be given in the formula by which funds are allocated to schools in order to provide more resources for children with special educational needs, but accurate targeting of such additional finance is problematic. The situation is rather more straightforward for the pupils who have statements, where resources are allocated to them as individuals. However, for those both with and without statements, the impact of local management of schools put adverse pressure on the resourcing of LEA support and advisory services (Diamond 1993; Lee and Henkhuzens 1996), and there is little doubt that it made more difficult the LEAs' task of planning, guiding and monitoring coherent services for pupils with special educational needs (Vincent et al. 1995).

Overall, the 1988 Act introduced some potential benefits for children with special educational needs, notably in the right of access to a broader range of learning experiences than they had often received in the past. But at the same time it raised a great many concerns about the priority that can be given to special educational provision in the context of competitiveness between schools. It is precisely in the area of academic competition that those with special educational needs are most disadvantaged. There was anxiety therefore that they would become marginalized and that the gains made under the 1981 Education Act would be lost.

Many authors provided evidence to add weight to these concerns, including for example: a reported reduction in mainstream staffing to support special educational needs and a slowing down of inclusion initiatives (Clark et al. 1997); increasing referrals for statements (Davie 1996); and rising numbers of permanent exclusions (Garner 1993; Parsons and Howlett 1996).

It was against this background that the government initiated an Audit Commission/HMI investigation (1992) into the state of special educational provision across the country. The findings highlighted the lack of clarity and consistency in identifying special educational needs and in determining school and LEA roles and responsibilities, as well as problems in resourcing and statementing practice. This investigation was followed by the introduction of the 1993 Education Act and the Code of Practice (DfE 1994a).

The 1993 and 1996 Education Acts and the Code of Practice

Section III of the 1993 Education Act was concerned with special education, and, when enacted, it replaced almost all of the 1981 Act. In its turn, the 1993 Act together with the remaining part of the 1981 Act were replaced by the 1996 Education Act, Part IV of which deals with special educational needs. The Code of Practice, which was introduced by the 1993 Act, is not a piece of legislation, but a set of 'practical guidance' for schools and LEAs concerning their responsibilities. It aims to promote greater clarity and consistency in their practice and they are legally bound to 'have regard' to its provisions.

Definitions of special educational need and provision

The legal definitions of special educational need and provision remain as they were in the 1981 Act. The Code of Practice emphasizes that there is a continuum of need and a continuum of provision, and that children with special educational needs 'require the greatest possible access to a broad and balanced education, including the National Curriculum' (DfE 1994a: para. 1:2).

The role of ordinary schools

The statutory requirement on LEAs to educate children with special educational needs in ordinary schools is hedged with the same provisos as in the 1981 Act, but it is made clear in the Code of Practice that the needs of most should be met within mainstream education. Indeed, the emphasis of the Code is placed to such an extent on mainstream practice that special schools have frequently not recognized that it also applies to their provision (Lewis *et al.* 1996). All schools are required to develop special educational needs (SEN) policies, to make these available to parents and to report on their effectiveness at annual governors' meetings. They must identify someone, usually referred to as the special educational needs coordinator, or SENCO, who has responsibility for the day-to-day operation of that policy. This role, which is seen as a key to effective provision, is outlined more fully in Chapter 7. Elements which must be included in school policies are specified by regulations and elaborated in a government circular (DfE 1994b, 1994c). They include factual information about the coordination of provision in school, the guiding principles and objectives which underpin the school's policy, the way in which the Code of Practice is implemented, and arrangements for partnerships with parents, other schools and support services. Annual governors' meetings must also outline the arrangements the school makes for the admission of children with disabilities, the facilities provided to assist their access and the steps taken to ensure that they are not treated less favourably than other pupils.

Identification and assessment procedures

The Code of Practice gives detailed attention to the school-based assessment procedures that should be followed for the majority of children with special educational needs who do not require statements. It emphasizes the importance of early identification and outlines a continuous and progressive cycle of assessment, planning, action and review, which is characterized by partnerships between school staff and parents, and with other professionals as appropriate. It also highlights the need to involve the children themselves throughout the process. The framework that it sets out is described in more detail in Chapter 3, and the development of Individual Educational Plans (IEPs) for children with special educational needs is discussed in Chapter 5. There is no requirement that children must be taken through all the school-based elements of this framework prior to a referral for statutory assessment. However, in an attempt to achieve greater consistency, the Code sets out some general guidance on when children with particular forms of special educational need might be considered for a statement.

The formal statutory assessment procedures themselves are set out at length in the 1996 Act. They are essentially similar to those laid down by the 1981 Act, but strengthen parental rights in the process and include both a time limit, normally of 26 weeks, and also a requirement for greater specificity in the drawing up of statements. The procedures should be initiated when the LEA has grounds to believe that additional or special resources will be needed to meet a child's educational needs. Although this should not be the first indication to parents that their child is experiencing difficulties, and indeed they can themselves request an assessment, the LEA must inform them in writing of its intention to begin the procedures. In doing so, it should provide information about what is involved and about the rights of parents to put forward their views. It should also give the name of an LEA officer who can provide them with further details. Parents have 29 days to respond, and the LEA must take account of their views in deciding whether or not to proceed. At all stages, parents are to be kept informed of the decisions that are made. When assessment does go ahead, the LEA must seek advice from all relevant professionals, including, for example, those from health and social service departments, as well as from education. Following this, the LEA determines whether there is a case for special provision to be made. If so, it has to draft a statement and send this, together with copies of the professional advice, to the parents. If not, it must send parents notice giving full reasons for the decision: the Code of Practice recommends that this should preferably take the form of a 'note in lieu', written with the same care as a draft statement.

The draft statement outlines the LEA's assessment of the child's needs and specifies the provision that it proposes to make to meet those needs. At this stage, LEAs must also explain to parents how they can express a preference for a particular school for their child, and the procedures available to them if they disagree with part or all of the draft statement. Their stated preference of school should be accepted, unless the school is judged unsuitable to meet the child's needs or it would not be compatible with the effective education of other pupils or the efficient use of resources. The LEA must, of course, consult with a school's governing body before naming it on a child's statement. In the event of any disagreement, the LEA must take parental views into account before deciding on the final statement. Figure 2.1 (see pp. 36–7) illustrates the form a statement can take: parental representations and professional assessment advice should also be attached as appendices.

The final statement is sent to the parents together with the name of a 'Named Person' to whom they can go for information and advice, and an explanation of appeal procedures. The Named Person is ideally someone independent of the LEA, and the Code of Practice recommends that where possible he or she is identified by the parents and LEA before the assessment process begins, rather than only at this point. If parents disagree with an LEA decision not to issue a statement or with the final version of the statement when one is drawn up, then they have the right of appeal to an Independent Special Educational Needs Tribunal. Once statements are maintained, they must be reviewed at least annually, and from the point where pupils reach the age of 14 years reviews should begin to focus on coordinated planning for their transition to post-school options. Parents must be informed of any changes which are proposed to their child's statement and also have the right to request the LEA to undertake reassessments.

Parental involvement in the decision-making process

The 1993 Education Act and the Code of Practice have been described as a re-endorsement of the principles of the Warnock Report (e.g. Stakes and Hornby 1997) and they are certainly characterized by a strengthening of the parental role in educational decision-making. Parents' groups have responded positively to the changes that were introduced (e.g. Friel 1997). As might be anticipated, they welcomed the access to a Named Person who could provide advice and support to enable them to take up their rights, and to the Independent Special Educational Needs Tribunal if needed, as well as the strong emphasis that the Code places on consultation and partnership. Russell (1997) reports that parents have also appreciated the more systematic and consistent approach adopted for children without statements as a result of the implementation of the Code.

The impact of the Code of Practice

At a school level, the Code of Practice has in theory provided an impetus for a fresh look at the approach taken to parental involvement, but in practice the priority in many cases has been the development of within-school systems for assessment, decision-making and review. Some schools have been slow to begin to explore the ways in which they might involve parents in these, and few parents have been made aware of their school's SEN policies (Beveridge 1997). The impact of the Code on procedures within school, however, has typically been reported as positive, with

OFSTED (1996) finding that it had served to raise awareness of special educational needs and to improve the quality of provision. Some concerns have been aired: for example, that the emphasis of the Code is more on intervention than on the prevention of learning difficulties, and that in raising the profile of children with special educational needs there is a risk of greater labelling and emphasis on difference from their peers (Sewell 1996; Clark *et al.* 1997). Nevertheless, a consistent picture emerges from a range of different studies (e.g. Loxley and Bines 1995; DfEE 1997b; Lewis *et al.* 1997; Bowers *et al.* 1998) that the principles of the Code have been well accepted among SENCOs, who have welcomed both the clarification and focus it provides for school policy and procedures, and also the enhanced definition and status attached to their role.

In terms of the practicalities involved, there is no doubt that the Code makes heavy demands of SENCOs, and it is essential that they have the full support of governors and senior management if they are to fulfil their role most effectively. The most frequently raised criticisms have focused on the bureaucratic nature of the planning and review procedures, the competing pressures of the diverse elements of the role and the lack of dedicated time for undertaking these. The government has acknowledged these concerns and has expressed the intention of reducing the amount of paperwork involved when it introduces a revised Code in the school year 2000/2001.

At an authority-wide level, inconsistencies remain in statementing procedures and the proportions of children with statements vary from fewer than 2 per cent to over 4 per cent in different LEAs (DfEE 1997a). Across the country as a whole, these proportions have continued to rise, leading to less clarity about the boundary between those with and without statements and therefore more potential scope for argument and disagreement. This has led in turn to increasing concerns about the inequities that can result from parental lobbying on behalf of their own children and the confrontational approach which can characterize the use of the Independent Tribunal. Gross (1996), for example, has presented evidence that it is the most articulate and best supported parents who are gaining additional resources for their children through statementing. Some believe that the way forward is to provide advocacy for all parents who want this (e.g. Simmons 1996), but others fear that, in a time of financial constraint, such an approach continues to focus resources on the minority at the expense of the majority of children with special educational needs. There is therefore a growing body of opinion that there is a need to re-think the whole question of whether statements represent the best means of ensuring resources for children with special educational need (e.g. Williams and Maloney 1998).

Given the current approach to resource allocation, it is inevitable that there will continue to be cases where disagreements between LEAs and parents require the mediation of the Tribunal for their resolution. However, parental recourse to the Tribunal is sometimes associated with misunderstandings arising from a lack of clear and sufficient information, and it has been noted that almost a third of appeals are withdrawn if parents are given access to independent information, advice and support (Russell 1996). It might be anticipated, therefore, that an increased use of independent advice together with the Parent Partnership schemes which have been developed in many LEAs (e.g. Trier 1997) should help to prevent unnecessary confrontation. Such an approach has been accepted by the government, which has stated its intention that, from 1999, all LEAs should have Parent Partnership schemes in place through which they are to make 'Independent Parental Supporters' (a development of the Named Person role) available to all parents of children with special educational needs. They are also expected to establish conciliation procedures which have an independent component, in order to try to resolve any disputes.

Both the proposed revision to the Code of Practice and also these initiatives in LEA support for parents were first outlined in a Green Paper (DfEE 1997a) which the government described as launching the 'most far-reaching review' of special education since the publication of the Warnock Report. The Green Paper together with the 'programme of action' (DfEE 1998a) which followed it set the scene for continuing developments to the legislative and policy frameworks which will govern provision. In the following brief overview, some of the main elements are outlined.

Continuing developments

The Secretary of State for Education has argued that 'We must develop inclusive schools if we want to lay the foundations for an inclusive society' (Blunkett 1997: 150). The Green Paper (DfEE 1997a) provides a strong endorsement of the principles of inclusion on moral and social as well as educational grounds. Other key themes concern: the maintenance of high expectations for children with special educational needs; the support and empowerment of their parents; a shifting of resources to allow a greater focus on early intervention and prevention; the promotion of inter-agency collaboration; and the need for staff development to meet special educational needs.

The Green Paper describes an aim to reduce the numbers of children identified as having special educational needs from an estimated 18 per cent of the school population to a figure closer to 10 per cent, through a range of early intervention initiatives, and also through the impact of target-setting, both at school and LEA levels. For children identified as having special educational needs, it highlights an intention to strengthen the school-based stages of the Code of Practice in order to reduce the proportion requiring statements. It does not raise the immediate prospect of radical change to the statementing process, but focuses instead on the need to improve procedures for drawing up and reviewing statements.

The vast majority of responses to the Green Paper have been positive concerning the principle of promoting greater inclusion, although many reservations have also been aired about the practicalities and resource implications that are involved. There is a general consensus too concerning the need for enhanced inter-agency collaboration and staff development opportunities, and widespread support for the emphasis given to early intervention. Early intervention is described in the Green Paper as 'the best way to tackle educational disadvantage' (DfEE 1997a: 12), and Norwich (1998) is among those who have voiced concerns that no clear distinction is made here between educational needs which can be prevented, those which can be ameliorated and those which will need continued special support throughout the years of school. The need for such a distinction does not only apply to the question of what can be achieved through early intervention but more generally to the issue of what might constitute realistically high expectations. There is no doubt that children with special educational needs can be limited by the low expectations that are held of them, and it is important therefore that they are included to the greatest extent possible in initiatives that are designed to raise achievement: currently, this encompasses, for example, their involvement in the national literacy and numeracy strategies, as discussed in Chapter 4, as well as in target-setting by schools and LEAs. However, the targets that are set for raising achievement must be relevant to children with the full range of needs, and go beyond an emphasis on narrowly defined academic attainments. If they do not, then these initiatives can pull against the principles of inclusion the government seeks to promote (Farrell 1998).

It is the Green Paper's reference to reducing the proportion of statements which has caused most debate. Lunt (1998), for example, has emphasized that what is required is an approach which rewards schools for meeting needs and where progress is seen as a move away from, rather than towards, the maintenance of a statement. She describes the Green Paper as offering the opportunity to take a radical look at how the education system as a whole can better respond to pupil diversity. By contrast, parents and parent organizations have understandably seen the proposal as a potential threat to the safeguarding of resources to meet their children's needs. Their concerns have been crystallized by Simmons (1998), who has argued that any notion of a fixed percentage in the number of statements that are maintained signals a move away from a 'needs-led' approach to the sort of 'discretionary, resource-led' arrangement which must act to the disadvantage of parents and their children.

Following consultation on the Green Paper, the government set out its 'programme of action' for special educational provision (DfEE 1998a). This emphasizes that parents need access to independent advice and 'a powerful say in the way their child is educated' (ibid.: 11), and it introduces the expectations of LEAs in relation to Parent Partnership schemes and Independent Parental Supporters that were referred to earlier in this chapter. It also confirms that the government's early intervention initiatives, such as Early Excellence Centres, set up to develop multi-agency early years services, and Sure Start projects, targeted at areas of social disadvantage to work with parents to promote their children's development, will give priority to children with special educational needs and their families.

The main features of the existing framework for special educational provision are to be retained, including the definition of what constitutes special educational need. As discussed in the previous chapter, the view that fresh consideration should be given to the sorts of educational need regarded as 'special' has gained support in recent years. The government has acknowledged that the term 'special educational need' can be used differently by schools and LEAs, but nevertheless has decided to keep to the legal definition that has been in use since the 1981 Education Act. The principles of the Code of Practice also remain in place, although the Code itself is to be revised to include further guidance, for example in relation to the development of Individual Educational Plans (IEPs). Structurally, a major change which is in line with the aim of reducing the number of children identified as having special educational needs is the proposed removal of Stage 1 from the school-based elements of the Code. This change is discussed in more detail in Chapter 3. With respect to statements, the government has responded to the concerns expressed by parents and their representatives by providing reassurance that it will not limit access to statutory assessment procedures or remove the legal protection offered by a statement. Nevertheless, it reaffirms in the programme of action that its aim over time is to reduce the reliance on statements and to emphasize the role of the school-based elements of the Code in meeting children's needs.

A strengthening of the school-based elements requires clarification of the relative roles and responsibilities of schools and LEAs. The government has promoted the idea of further financial delegation from LEAs to schools. Such a move may well give schools more scope for the development of their provision, but there must be concerns about the extent to which further delegation is compatible with LEA capacity to maintain effective support services. It seems evident that a coherent policy between schools and LEAs, characterized by transparency and mutual accountability, is needed. The new framework for the local management of schools introduced in 1999 goes some way towards this in its requirement that LEAs publish a budget statement for each school and, within this, identify the part of the budget that has been allocated for special educational provision. Important though questions of resourcing for support are, a strengthening of the school role in meeting special educational needs must be seen to be fundamentally related to staff commitment and a whole school approach. The additional help that children with special educational needs require in order to overcome their learning difficulties is only likely to be safeguarded when they are afforded equal status and value to their peers. This requires positive attitudes among all staff and a determination to promote the educational opportunities of all their pupils.

A whole school commitment to the needs of all pupils is, of course, essential if a more inclusive educational framework is to be achieved. In the programme of action the government reiterates the commitment to inclusive education that was spelt out in the Green Paper. It envisages:

> an inclusive local educational system in which the normal presumption is that children spend as much time as possible in a mainstream setting; and where, when a special school (or other specialist provision) is right for a child, it has clear links with neighbouring mainstream schools.
>
> (DfEE 1998a: 23)

In these words it makes clear that special schools continue to have a significant role to play, but at the same time it emphasizes the need for planned interaction between special and mainstream schools. Furthermore, it holds out the prospect that the legal requirement on LEAs to educate children with special educational needs in mainstream schools may be strengthened in the future. In the meantime, from 1999 LEAs are required to publish information in their Education Development Plans about both their strategies for raising the achievements of children with special educational needs and also their policies on inclusion. The issues involved in developing effective inclusive practice are addressed in the next chapter.

Discussion points

1   How far should the education of children with special educational needs in ordinary schools be regarded as an equal opportunities issue? Consider the role of staff attitudes and

commitment in developing a positive whole school approach to special educational provision.

2   Children with special educational needs are almost inevitably disadvantaged in an ethos of academic competitiveness. Yet it can be argued that an emphasis on non-academic aspects of their achievements leads to lowered expectations and restricted educational opportunities. With these points in mind, consider the main issues involved in ensuring that the targets set for raising achievement are relevant for children with special educational needs.

3   Statements: an important safeguard of resources for those with the greatest needs, or an unnecessary way of categorizing children? What do you see as the main advantages and limitations of the statementing process?

Further reading

Friel, J. (1997) *Children with Special Needs: Assessment, Law and Practice: Caught in the Act*, 4th edn, London: Jessica Kingsley.

Stakes, R. and Hornby, G. (1997) *Change in Special Education*, London: Cassell.

Part 1 Introduction

(specifies details of child's name, date of birth and address, home language and religion; parents'/carers' names and addresses)

Part 2 Special Educational Needs

'Child X 's learning difficulties are in:

> spoken language and social interaction;
> maintaining concentration;
> literacy skills;
> numeracy skills.'*

Part 3 Special Educational Provision

Objectives:

> 'To develop spoken language and social skills;
> To extend concentration span;
> To improve basic literacy skills;
> To improve basic numeracy skills.'

Educational provision to meet needs and objectives:
'Access to the full National Curriculum without modification, at an appropriate level as part of a normal class group, with:

1 implementation of small group programmes to develop social and communication skills;
2 implementation of individual programme to develop concentration span;
3 individual and teacher-directed small group provision to develop literacy skills;
4 individual and teacher-directed small group provision to develop numeracy skills;

continued overleaf

5 in-class support to help child X's access to the curriculum (1 and 5 require n hours daily Learning Support Assistant time, provided on a small group basis);
6 close home/school liaison.'

Monitoring:
'Targets for each objective identified on IEPs drawn up in consultation with parents and specialist learning support teacher and reviewed termly.'*

Part 4 Placement

(specifies type and name of school or other arrangements where provision is to be made)

Part 5 Non-educational Needs

(specifies any needs such as medical which should be addressed)

Part 6 Non-educational Provision

(specifies the provision which is to be made to meet these needs, its objectives and monitoring arrangements)

Figure 2.1 An example of the format for a statement of special educational needs

Note *The examples given in Parts 2 and 3 are not verbatim extracts from one child's statement, but are illustrative of the sorts of need and provision that may be specified.

Chapter 3

The range of special educational need and provision

Special educational need arises from a complex interaction of personal and environmental factors, and may be viewed as a mismatch between the emotional, social and learning demands that are made of a pupil and the resources that the pupil has to meet these demands. It follows, therefore, that the difficulties a pupil experiences cannot be understood in isolation from the context in which they occur. In the majority of cases, special educational need is identified at school, when aspects of a pupil's progress or behaviour give cause for concern. Because educational needs are relative to the learning contexts that pupils experience, and to the attitudes and expectations of others, teacher judgements about pupils are likely to be affected by the general levels of attainment in a class, as well as by school and LEA practice. Curricular and organizational factors contribute to the extent to which children experience difficulties at school. Furthermore, it is clear that gender, home background, socio-economic and ethnic variables are also often associated with the process of identification of special educational need. Thus, while within-child factors can play an important part in learning or behavioural difficulties, these should not be seen in isolation from the contribution of home, school and wider social influences.

Nevertheless, for a minority of pupils the assessment of special educational need is based primarily on the diagnosis of some specific impairment which restricts their ability to participate fully in the educational opportunities that are generally available. It is important, therefore, that teachers are aware of the nature of such impairments. Usually, although not always, these are likely to have been detected prior to a child starting school. More boys than girls are likely to be affected, but, unlike the larger categories of special educational need, the presence of specific impairment is not associated with particular socio-economic variables.

Specific forms of impairment

It is important to emphasize that the relationship between a particular impairment and a child's educational needs is not a straightforward one. Any significant impairment gives rise to certain disabilities or limitations, but the extent to which these 'handicap' the child will depend on his or her strengths as well as weaknesses, and will also reflect the degree of support and understanding that is provided at home, at school and in the community more generally. As a result, a wide range of variation can be described in both the needs and educational progress that are experienced by children who have similar levels of impairment. It is clear, however, that close cooperation and liaison between home, school and other involved professionals is vital if their needs are to be most effectively met. In the following discussion, attention is drawn to some of the main forms of impairment that teachers may meet in ordinary schools, but it should be stressed that this does not represent a comprehensive overview. Furthermore, although these have been categorized as sensory, physical, cognitive and medical, it is important to note that there may often be an overlap between these impairments, and it is not always easy to distinguish which is the more significant in terms of its educational implications.

Sensory impairments

Complete loss of either hearing or vision is rare, but any significant degree of impairment involving these senses restricts the means by which children are able to integrate their experiences and make sense of their environments. As a result, they may find their learning contexts less predictable and secure than they appear to others. There is, of course, likely to be variation in acuity of hearing and vision within any class, and some of the management implications that result from the presence of pupils with diagnosed sensory impairments, such as attention to lighting, noise level, physical organization and flexible modes of instruction, may well benefit others in the group.

It is estimated that about one in a thousand children have a severe hearing loss, and almost two more in each thousand have a loss which requires the use of an aid (Bishop and Gregory 1986). Less severe and intermittent losses, which are far more frequent, can play a significant part in many children's educational difficulties. Hearing impairment can be described as 'sensorineural' or 'conductive'. The first term refers to a loss resulting from damage to the inner ear or auditory nerve and associated brain cells. This is usually irreversible, and in about half of all cases it is thought to be attributable to genetic factors. Other causes include maternal contraction of German measles in the early months of pregnancy, as well as childhood viral infections such as meningitis. By contrast, conductive hearing losses result from some blockage or damage to the outer or middle ear, and these are usually both less severe and also more likely to be treatable. The most common cause is the middle ear infection often referred to as 'glue ear', which occurs and can recur during childhood. This leads to fluctuating levels of hearing which, if not detected, are likely to affect both language acquisition and general progress at school. It is not uncommon to find that children have been labelled as 'uncooperative', 'lazy' or 'inattentive' because of unnoticed hearing losses and it is, therefore, very important that teachers are alert to any signs that a pupil may not be hearing adequately. It cannot be assumed that the child will draw explicit attention to the difficulties that arise as, particularly in the early years of schooling, children may not be able to monitor such changes in their hearing acuity for themselves.

The majority of children with hearing impairment are educated in ordinary schools, where, particularly in cases of severe loss, they and their teachers should receive some support from specialist peripatetic teachers. The nature of that support will vary according to individual needs, but is likely to include guidance on how to maximize the use of the hearing that a child does have, as well as on the development of appropriate communication strategies. Whether or not children require hearing aids, the acoustics of the room, the level of background noise, their positioning for full class and group activities, and the clarity with which their teachers communicate will all affect how successfully they can use their hearing. A number of different forms of aid may be used which act to amplify those sounds that the child is capable of hearing. Conventional aids pick up all the sounds within a limited range, and amplify most of those that are nearest to the wearer. By contrast, radio-microphone aids allow for the selective amplification of the voice of a teacher who is wearing a microphone, and operate over a much greater distance. In some cases, a loop system may be installed round the perimeter of a room which enables a better quality of sound to be received by those wearing aids.

There has been a long-standing debate about which means of communication should be the primary focus in teaching children with severe hearing impairments (see, for example, Gregory *et al.* 1998 for a discussion of the issues involved). Some favour oral methods which emphasize the medium of the spoken word, whereas others advocate the use of signing. British Sign Language is the natural language of the deaf community in Britain, and in recent years it has increasingly been argued that it should be regarded as a first language by those teaching deaf children. A further approach, known as Total Communication, which has also gained in popularity, seeks to combine speech and signing together with other non-verbal aspects of communication.

The major educational disadvantage for children with hearing impairment derives from limitations in their language experiences. The potential effects of unresolved difficulties in this area are wide-ranging, involving personal, social and cognitive aspects of their learning at school (Webster and Wood 1989). A fundamental need for children with such impairments, therefore, is the fullest possible opportunities to develop their communication skills, using whatever residual hearing and other means that are available to help them.

Unlike hearing impairment, significant visual impairment is comparatively rare among children of school age. Its cause is not always known but it may either be present from birth or be acquired subsequently. Assessment of the extent of impairment is based on measured acuity after correction with lenses, and also takes account of any restriction in the field of vision. Children who are partially sighted can, with help, use print in their learning and thus their educational needs are primarily concerned with the use of aids and materials to assist this means of access to the school curriculum. Those who are assessed as blind will usually have some light reception and may have further residual sight which can be used, but they are unable to read print of any size. They therefore require alternatives, such as Braille, tactile maps and diagrams and 'talking books' (recorded on to audiotape), if they are to participate fully in the curriculum. They are also likely to need special help in order to develop their orientation and independent mobility in the environment. Although practice varies from LEA to LEA, visually impaired children have increasingly been educated in ordinary schools. Where this is so, they and their teachers should be supported by specialist teachers of the visually impaired. These staff can provide guidance on lighting, materials and the use of specific aids in the classroom. They may also work individually with pupils; for example, to develop their skills in Braille. When such specialist input is necessary, it is important that there is close liaison and joint planning with class teachers in order to ensure that it is incorporated as far as possible into the pupil's broader experiences of the curriculum.

The loss of vision has implications for a number of aspects of learning. For example, communication may be hampered where children have difficulty in picking up non-verbal cues, and active interaction with the environment may also be inhibited. Furthermore, reading, whether by Braille or from magnified print, is a laborious and lengthy process. It is important, therefore, that teachers give attention to the timing of tasks which require such reading, and that they also draw on a variety of alternative media, both auditory and tactile, to support the pupils' learning (Mason 1995). Where vision is the only area of impairment, with appropriate help and support children are generally reported to achieve levels of attainment similar to those of their sighted peers, although they may need longer in order to do so.

Physical impairment

Explicit attention to the educational needs that are associated with poorly developed motor coordination will be necessary in any classroom group. Henderson and Sugden (1991), for example, estimate that up to 15 per cent of pupils have a degree of physical impairment which can interfere with their progress at school. Among these will be a large number of pupils who appear physically 'normal', but who have considerable difficulty in tasks which involve the planning and coordination of motor tasks. Often referred to in the past as 'clumsy', they may now be described as having dyspraxia or developmental coordination disorder (Sugden and Wright 1998). There is a wide range of individual variation among the children concerned: some may experience difficulty with fine motor skills, such as handwriting and drawing, some with gross motor skills, for example in P.E. and games, and some with the planning and coordination of speech. If their needs are not recognized, their self-confidence, social relationships and behaviour can also be affected. Depending on the pattern and severity of their difficulties, physiotherapists, occupational therapists or speech and language therapists may be involved in planning intervention, which is likely to involve regular short bursts of practice at home and at school on the tasks which cause particular difficulty.

Where pupils have a more specific physical impairment, their ability to interact with the environment will be limited in some way. However, because of the diversity of such impairments, it is difficult to generalize about the nature of the special needs that are likely to arise. On the whole, if their impairment is limited to particular muscles or limbs, then children's needs are primarily likely to be for therapy and care, together with special means of access to the curriculum. By contrast, where there is neurological damage, as for example in cerebral palsy and spina bifida, this can lead to additional sensory and learning difficulties.

The term cerebral palsy refers to a group of movement disorders resulting from damage to the developing brain. This damage is usually associated with trauma at around the time of birth, such as a lack of oxygen to the brain, although less often damage may occur later. The most common forms of cerebral palsy are spasticity, characterized by stiff movements of the affected limbs, and athetosis, which results in writhing or jerky involuntary movements. The extent and severity of the motor impairment vary widely, as does the degree of any additional difficulty. Vision, hearing and speech articulation can be affected, and there is an increased likelihood of epilepsy. Intellectual functioning may also be impaired, although this is not necessarily the case, and the educational attainments of some children with cerebral palsy are at least as high as those of their able-bodied contemporaries.

Spina bifida is a condition in which damage occurs to the spinal cord during pregnancy. The resulting physical difficulties range from mild to severe. This depends on the location and extent of the damage, for it affects the child's control of his or her body below that point. As a result, children with spina bifida can often have limited or no use of their lower limbs and may be incontinent. Many also have hydrocephalus, a build-up of cerebro-spinal fluid in the ventricles of the brain, which if unchecked can lead to further damage, but which is usually controlled by the insertion of a valve or 'shunt' to drain the fluid into the bloodstream. As with cerebral palsy, the full range of cognitive competence is found among children affected by spina bifida, although it has been reported that those with hydrocephalus often have additional learning difficulties (Henderson and Sugden 1991).

It can be seen, then, that different forms of physical impairment may lead to a variety of individual needs. Special physical and health needs, such as for physiotherapy or help with mobility and continence, require liaison and coordination between teachers and other professionals. One area for consideration here is likely to be the balance between time spent in meeting such needs and that which is necessary to ensure that a pupil has the opportunity to participate in the full range of general curricular activities. Modification of task materials and the use of special aids or equipment may be required to help pupils engage with these activities, and more time may be needed to allow for the completion of tasks. Attention to the physical layout of the classroom will also be required, for this will need to be designed to maximize ease of movement and access to resources. At the same time, though, the presence of additional aids and equipment will have implications for the way in which available space can be most effectively managed. Furthermore, adaptations may be necessary throughout a school, for example to doors and stairways, in order to facilitate mobility and access for pupils with physical impairments.

Cognitive and other impairments

By comparison with the sorts of impairment so far discussed, the identification of causes of cognitive limitations is far less straightforward. In some cases, cognitive impairment can be associated with genetic factors and maternal conditions during pregnancy, such as infections, diet and drug use, as well as with birth complications and subsequent childhood illness and injury. However, it is also evident that environmental influences play a significant part, and that the interaction of within-child and environmental factors is complex. As a result, early developmental delays and difficulties may often prove to be temporary, and even where they persist it is frequently not possible to identify a specific cause.

Among the minority of children with persistent and generalized delays in their development for whom specific causes have been identified, those with Down's syndrome stand out as the largest single group. This syndrome results from a chromosomal abnormality, usually in the form of an extra chromosome 21, and it is frequently associated with additional difficulties, among which the most common are heart defects and hearing loss. Although those with the syndrome share a number of distinctive physical characteristics, there is far wider diversity in their development than is sometimes appreciated. In the past, a diagnosis of Down's syndrome was very often taken to imply 'severe subnormality' (and thus, prior to 1970, 'ineducability'), but there has been an increasing recognition of individual variation in the nature and extent of their educational needs. That is, while some children do experience severe learning difficulties, the difficulties of others have been assessed as moderate or mild. As a result, more children with Down's syndrome are being educated in ordinary schools and individual educational attainments at GCSE level have recently been reported. Early educational intervention may do much to promote their development and learning, and with appropriate help some children with Down's syndrome have acquired reading skills prior to starting school (Buckley et al. 1996). Overall, it seems evident that there is much still to be learned about the full range of educational outcomes which may be achieved. The cognitive difficulties of children with Down's syndrome are generally reported to lie primarily in consolidating and generalizing their skills, and where this is so they require carefully planned and structured activities to facilitate their learning (Stratford and Gunn 1996).

Very much rarer, but included here because the term has become a familiar one, is the diagnosis of autism. Although the precise causes of this severe and complex syndrome are still unclear, research evidence points to an impairment of cognitive functioning (Frith 1989). Autism is characterized by impairments in the development of social relationships, communication skills and imagination, and their educational needs are particularly associated with these areas of learning (Jordan and Powell 1995; Wing 1996). Children with autism are also typically described as showing inflexibility in aspects of their behaviour which may become ritualized into fixed routines. Their speech can be echolalic (repeating what has been heard), and the use of eye contact, gestural or facial expression as well as the timing of conversational turn-taking may all be affected. They often demonstrate a rather limited awareness of the intentions or moods of others and appear to have difficulty in making sense of their social environment. There is a wide range of variation among children with autism, and, although most have significant and often severe learning difficulties, some demonstrate exceptional skills in a specific area of development, such as in music, art or mathematical calculation. Recently, there has been an increase in the diagnosis of a particular form of autism known as Asperger syndrome. While children with this syndrome have impairments in their social, communicative and imaginative skills, these tend to be less marked, and they do not generally have other significant learning difficulties. The term 'autistic spectrum disorders' is often used to include both autism and Asperger syndrome. Children with autism have traditionally been taught in special schools or units, although increasingly some have been placed in ordinary classes with support. Those with Asperger syndrome are often educated in mainstream schools.

One childhood disorder which is frequently associated with behaviour, but which has a strong cognitive component, is Attention Deficit Disorder/Attention Deficit with Hyperactivity Disorder (ADD/ADHD). Its diagnosis is based on difficulties in sustaining attention and controlling impulses and, in the case of ADHD, hyperactivity. There has recently been a large increase in the number of children diagnosed, and it is estimated that between 3 and 5 per cent of children may be affected (Cooper and Ideus 1995), most of whom are educated in ordinary schools. They experience chronic and persistent difficulties in responding to classroom tasks and routines, and often demonstrate low self-esteem. Some children are prescribed medication intended to aid concentration and reduce impulsiveness and

over-activity, and their parents can be involved in behaviour management programmes at home. Classroom-based interventions, which
may be supported by educational psychologists or specialist teachers,
typically focus on helping the children develop skills for organizing
and managing their own learning behaviour.

Cognitive and language development are inter-related in important ways, and therefore it is not surprising to find that children
with cognitive impairments also typically show delays, and in some
cases disorders, in their language acquisition. As previously
discussed, such difficulties can also result from sensory impairments and, indeed, temporary language delays are not rare during
the early years of childhood. Infrequently, however, specific and
longer-lasting problems occur, not only in articulation but also
involving impairments in the interpretation of the sounds and
grammar of speech or in the communicative functions of language.
Where these difficulties are particularly severe, pupils tend to
receive at least part of their education in specially resourced provision. However, when it is felt that pupils will benefit from being
taught with peers who are competent language users, then they are
placed in ordinary classroom contexts. In such cases, with support
from speech and language therapists and/or specialist language
teachers, additional help and guidance will focus primarily on the
social use of language and appropriate communication strategies in
the classroom (Martin and Miller 1995).

Some children with language impairments may also have problems in acquiring literacy skills. The identification of such problems
is, of course, usually made at school. Reading difficulty is particularly prevalent among pupils with special educational needs, and
this is a reflection of both the importance attached to literacy and
also, as discussed later in this chapter, of the way in which educational progress is assessed. In many cases poor progress in reading
may be symptomatic of general difficulties in learning, but in others
it may provide evidence of a more specific educational need. That
is, some children experience significant difficulties in their reading
but not in other unrelated areas of their learning. Specific reading
difficulty is often referred to as dyslexia, although it is important to
note that some controversy surrounds the use of the term.
Definitions of what constitutes specific reading difficulty vary, and
so accordingly do estimates of its incidence. The Dyslexia Institute

suggests that as many as 1 in 25 children may be affected. It characterizes dyslexia as a distinctive pattern of learning difficulties that is particularly associated with the acquisition of phonological reading strategies. Others question whether these difficulties represent a specific 'condition' which gives rise to needs that are qualitatively different from those experienced by the larger number of children whose reading skills are delayed (e.g. Coltheart and Jackson 1998). What is not in doubt, however, is that there is a minority of pupils whose reading attainments are significantly below the standards they achieve in other areas of learning, and who, like others with more general difficulties, require help and support to both build on their strengths and to meet their particular needs.

Medical needs

Not all children with medical conditions have special educational needs, and it would be misleading to suggest that medical needs necessarily represent a form of specific impairment. Nevertheless, where a child's medical condition limits access to education in significant ways, then it clearly acts as an impairment to learning. Circular 14/96 (DfEE 1996b) advises that certain conditions may require an individual health care plan to be drawn up by school staff in liaison with health professionals, in order to ensure a child's safety in school. Equally important is the need for planning which focuses on issues of curricular access and of social and emotional well-being. Chronic illness often results in frequent interruptions to schooling, which, unless properly recognized, monitored and compensated for, are likely to lead to gaps in children's knowledge which affect their future learning. Bolton (1997) has provided a vivid picture of the ways in which children's confidence in their ability to understand and deal with classroom demands can be undermined if they are absent when routines and procedures are introduced. They may also experience difficulties in maintaining and developing classroom friendships. As a consequence, the disruption to their schooling can affect social, emotional and academic progress. There is an evident need for close liaison between school staff and parents, and with any home tutors, hospital teachers or health professionals involved, in order to minimize the risk of this occurring.

The relationship between specific impairments and special educational needs

Clark and her colleagues (Clark *et al*. 1997) are among those who have drawn attention to the rise in the identification of particular categories of specific learning difficulty, such as dyslexia and ADHD, in recent years. They express concerns that an increased emphasis on syndromes focuses attention on within-child deficits and away from the interactive nature of the resulting special educational needs. It is important, therefore, in concluding this discussion of specific forms of impairment, to reiterate, first, that there is wide variation in the impact these have on individual children. Second, although this variation is in part determined by the severity and extent of impairment, it is also significantly affected by the quality of the learning experiences that are provided. Where the nature and extent of the child's difficulties are such that additional or special help will be required at school, then following formal assessment procedures a statement of special educational need should be provided by the LEA.

The wIder range of special educational need

The identification of special educational need is only associated with a diagnosis of specific impairment in a small percentage of cases. For most pupils with special educational needs, the difficulties that arise at school cannot be attributed to a particular impairment. Rather, these difficulties will involve some less easily defined lack of match between the pupils' personal resources and the demands that are made of them. Accordingly, the identification of special educational needs is primarily based on teacher judgement that a pupil's levels of attainment and/or behaviour are significantly poorer than those of the pupil's peers.

This means that both the incidence and nature of identified needs are fundamentally associated with the formal and informal assessment procedures that are used by teachers in school. Schools must all implement National Curriculum assessment procedures and, at primary level, baseline assessments. Beyond this, they vary in their systems for assessing and monitoring progress, but will typically use both teacher observation and also more standardized tests or curriculum-based checklists (Rouse and Agbenu 1998). Standardized tests have traditionally focused on 'basic skills' in reading, spelling and mathematics. In the junior schools studied by Croll and Moses in 1985, the predominant type of standardized assessment was some form of reading test: by far the largest category of special educational need identified by the teachers was learning difficulty (over 15 per cent of all pupils), and this was almost always characterized as involving problems in reading. The test scores of most of the children who were described as having such difficulties were at least twelve months below their chronological age, and for a minority they represented a delay in attainment of twenty-four months or more. However, it was not only the test scores which appeared to influence the teachers' judgements, as the identification of difficulty was also associated with the general reading standards in the class and with particular pupil characteristics. Thus younger children, boys and those whose behaviour was judged problematic were all more likely to be identified as having reading difficulties. Nearly all the pupils with reading difficulties were also regarded by their teachers as 'slow learners', but there were few references to other specific aspects of learning difficulty, such as in mathematics or problem-solving.

Since Croll and Moses undertook their study, the implementation of National Curriculum assessments has ensured that formal monitoring procedures go beyond measures of developing literacy. Nevertheless, there is little doubt that the assessment of reading attainment remains central to the identification of special educational need. This is not surprising, because reading is a skill which is highly valued by parents, schools and society, and furthermore it is a major means of access to many other aspects of the curriculum. Indeed, the recent introduction of the national literacy strategy reflects the continuing priority which it is given (DfEE 1998b). However, too often poor reading skills can lead to lowered expectations of a pupil's achievements in other areas of learning. For some pupils, their difficulties may be specific to reading, or, less frequently identified by schools, to other skill areas. Even where they experience generalized difficulties in their learning, though, they are still likely to demonstrate areas of relative strength and weakness across the curriculum.

It is important that assessment and monitoring procedures are used by teachers to draw attention to children's particular strengths as well as to pinpoint areas of weakness which require additional help. Through doing so, they can boost children's confidence in themselves as learners. By contrast, if difficulties in one aspect of learning lead to generalized expectations of low achievement across the curriculum, then a pupil's experiences of school are likely to be increasingly unrewarding. Successful learning makes considerable demands on children's personal resources. Anxiety or expectation of failure may often lead to a loss of motivation and self-esteem which can only compound the experience of learning difficulty. For this reason, it is not surprising that poor educational attainment is frequently associated with emotional or behavioural difficulties. It is important to stress, though, that the link between learning difficulty and emotional and behavioural difficulty is not inevitable. It is far less likely in situations where children feel supported and encouraged in their learning, are provided with real opportunities for success and, importantly, can see that their achievements are both recognized and valued.

Emotional and behavioural difficulties form the second largest category of special educational need identified in school, although it is unusual to find that this is the only type of difficulty a pupil experiences. The nature and extent of emotional and behavioural problems are wide-ranging and, apart from in the most severe cases, difficult to define. Teacher judgements are based on their professional experience and are likely to incorporate comparisons with the general standard of conduct in the class. Inevitably, though, they may also be influenced by personal values and expectations about 'appropriate' social and emotional behaviour. Typically, boys are more likely than girls to be identified as having emotional and behavioural difficulties, as are pupils from particular minority ethnic backgrounds (Daniels *et al.* 1996).

Any assessment of difficulty must take into account the interactive context in which it arises and, because teachers are so involved with that context, it can be difficult for them to analyse those aspects that may be contributing factors. Further, it has frequently been suggested that teachers are less alert to signs of emotional difficulty that create problems for the individual pupil than they are to the more overt behaviour that presents them with problems of class control. On the whole, it seems to be the case that pupils are identified by their teachers where their behaviour is judged to interfere with their own learning or that of other pupils, or to disrupt their relationships with peers and staff. Their needs are particularly associated with the social and emotional climate for learning as they experience it. They are fundamentally associated, therefore, with the quality of the relationships that the pupils are helped to develop in school. For this reason, there is a strong consensus of opinion that teachers can do much to alleviate their difficulties by adopting effective classroom management strategies which promote high levels of involvement in successful learning opportunities. These strategies are discussed in Chapter 6.

The identification of special educational need is not an end in itself, but should be the starting point for action to help pupils overcome their difficulties. The Code of Practice (DfE 1994a) introduced a staged process of assessment and intervention which begins with the class teacher but can subsequently involve increasing numbers of professionals, and which for a minority of pupils culminates in the provision of a statement of special educational need. Throughout all stages of the process, the special educational needs coordinator (SENCO) is responsible for keeping a record of identified needs on a special educational needs register. At the time of writing, there are three school-based stages of assessment, as follows:

1 *Stage 1.* A class teacher identifies concerns about a particular pupil and begins to undertake classroom-based observational assessment in order to explore the nature of the difficulties being experienced. At the same time he or she consults with the child's parents and seeks the child's own perspectives. Together with the SENCO, the teacher also gathers together relevant information from a range of sources, including school records of achievement, progress and behaviour as well as any information held in school from health, social services and other agencies. There is some evidence that the possible contribution of sensory, physical and health factors to difficulties in learning or behaviour can be underestimated by teachers, and it is therefore important that the accuracy of the available information from school records is checked. Once all the information has been collated it forms the basis for decisions about what sort of

help might be appropriate to meet the child's needs. Special help at Stage 1 typically takes the form of increased attention to the sorts of differentiation or class management approaches which might be effective. The child's progress is monitored and reviewed and, if difficulties persist then a decision will be made about whether to continue at Stage 1 or proceed to Stage 2.

2 *Stage 2.* The SENCO works with the child's teacher, and in consultation with parents, to plan more specific intervention. Stage 1 records and further classroom-based assessments are drawn upon to inform an Individual Education Plan (IEP) for the child. The IEP is used to identify specific targets for intervention, together with the learning activities, teaching methods, resources and organizational arrangements that are intended to help the child achieve these. The timespan for achieving targets, monitoring procedures and criteria for success is also outlined. Progress is regularly reviewed in order to ascertain whether it is appropriate to continue with the IEP or not. If the steps taken have not helped the child overcome his or her difficulties, then a decision may be taken to proceed to Stage 3.

3 *Stage 3.* At this stage, in addition to discussion with colleagues in school and with parents, the SENCO also draws on a wider range of support from outside school. Depending on the child's needs, this might include, for example, an educational psychologist, therapist or specialist advisory teacher. Stage 2 records are then supplemented by this additional assessment advice to form the basis for a further IEP. Monitoring and review procedures at Stage 3 become increasingly systematic and focused: if, as a result of review, it is judged that the school is not able to meet the child's needs within its existing resources and available levels of support, then it is at this point that the school will refer the pupil to the LEA to consider whether statutory assessment is needed, and if so, for this to be initiated.

The referral to the LEA represents Stage 4 of the Code of Practice. Children move onto Stage 5 when the LEA judges, on the basis of multiprofessional assessment and parental evidence, that it is necessary to draw up a statement of special educational needs. Although it is not necessary to go through each of the preceding school-based stages in order for a statement to be issued, in the majority of cases it is only when systematically planned and recorded interventions within school have failed to meet a child's needs that this stage is reached.

A revised Code of Practice is to be introduced in the school year 2000/2001. The government plans to reduce the number of school-based stages from three to two: it argues that many children at Stage 1 do not have identified special educational needs as defined in the legislation, and therefore should not be included within the provisions of the Code of Practice. It intends to offer separate guidance in relation to what will become a 'pre-Code' phase of concern about children's progress at school. At the same time it also proposes to move away from reference to 'stages', on the grounds that the term conveys the impression that the existing stages are 'a series of hurdles which children have to vault on their way to a statement, and even as a natural progression' (DfEE 1998a: 16). The revised Code is therefore anticipated to incorporate two school-based 'elements': *School Support* and *Support Plus*, which are broadly equivalent to the current Stages 2 and 3, respectively. A longer-term aim is to develop these in ways which allow a gradual decrease in the reliance on statements.

The range of special educational provision

Whether or not pupils have statements of special educational need, a generally accepted principle in determining appropriate provision is that, wherever possible, identified needs should be met without any unnecessary separation from their peers. The majority are, and have always been, educated in ordinary schools and, on the whole, the better the level and quality of provision that is available in regular classes, the more likely it is that most needs can be met there. Some would argue (e.g. Galloway 1985; Dessent 1987) that if an effective 'whole school approach' to special educational provision is developed then there is little justification for the separation of pupils into special groups, units or classes. Others, however (e.g. Norwich 1990), point out that such organizational arrangements can be beneficial to particular pupils, and are only likely to have negative consequences if they provide educational opportunities that are of lower quality and status than those available in ordinary classes.

The Warnock Committee identified four main types of special educational provision that might be made in ordinary schools:

(i)   'Full-time education in an ordinary class with any necessary help or support';
(ii) 'education in an ordinary class with periods of withdrawal to a special class or unit or other supporting base';
(iii) 'education in a special class or unit with periods of attendance at an ordinary class and full involvement in the general community life and extra-curricular activities of the ordinary school';
(iv) 'full-time education in a special class or unit with social contact with the main school'.

(DES 1978: para. 7.12)

In some respects these may be seen to form a continuum from ordinary to more specialized educational provision and can be extended further; first, to those special schools that have a variety of educational and social links with their neighbourhood schools, and finally to the small number that operate quite separately, including specialist residential provision. Variations on this continuum of provision continue to exist in most authorities to the present time. A number of authorities have established resourced mainstream schools with additional staffing and resourcing which enables them to provide a flexible mix of inclusive and more specialized provision for children with particular forms of special educational need. A further significant addition to special provision in most authorities since the implementation of the 1993 Education Act has been the introduction of pupil referral units (PRUs). In part a response to rising numbers of pupil exclusions (Garner 1994), PRUs typically focus on those pupils with emotional and behavioural difficulties who have been, or are at risk of being, excluded from mainstream schools. They work alongside mainstream schools, with the aim of returning pupils there wherever possible, as well as preparing older pupils for the transition to post-school life.

There is considerable variation between authorities in the numbers of pupils with statements of special educational need who are educated in ordinary or resourced mainstream schools. In some authorities, only a minority of statements are maintained for pupils in ordinary schools. By contrast, other authorities seek to educate children with statements in mainstream settings wherever possible. Across the country as a whole, a small increase in mainstream placement was recorded in the late 1980s (Swann 1992), but the trend appeared to be reversed, with a small increase in special school placement in the early 1990s (Norwich 1994). The current government has described the promotion of further inclusion as 'a cornerstone' of its strategy for children with special educational needs (DfEE 1998a): it has earmarked some financial support to provide an impetus for change and intends to require LEAs to include information about inclusion policy in their Education Development Plans. The decisions that are made at local level about the most appropriate provision for those with special educational needs are clearly influenced by the resources that are available. They are also fundamentally affected by the attitudes towards inclusive education that are held by LEAs, teachers, parents and, less frequently taken into account, the pupils themselves.

Inclusive educational provision

The term 'inclusion' is both widely used and also open to differing interpretations. It is helpful, therefore, to contrast it with earlier ways of characterizing what was previously referred to as 'integration'. The Warnock Committee distinguished between three main forms of integration: 'locational' integration occurs when special units or classes are attached to, or share a site with, ordinary schools; 'social' integration refers to situations where the unit's pupils 'eat, play and consort with other children, and possibly share organized out-of-classroom activities'; and 'functional' or the fullest form of integration is achieved if, in addition to social contacts, those with special educational needs join the regular school classes on a full- or part-time basis (DES 1978: paras 7.6 to 7.11).

This was, as the Committee acknowledged, a rather basic model, and it led to some over-simplified ways of conceptualizing integration. First, it encouraged greater attention to the question of where a child was placed than to the quality of the learning experiences that were provided. Second, it reinforced the notion that was then current that integration concerned only those children who had traditionally been educated in special schools. In the years following the publication of the Warnock Report, it became clear that both these aspects needed to be questioned.

The Fish Report for the Inner London Education Authority (ILEA) in 1985 represented an early emerging concern that integration must be conceptualized as a dynamic process rather than as a simple state of school placement. From this perspective integration implies 'continued and planned interaction with contemporaries' (ILEA 1985). In terms of Warnock's categorizations, locational or physical proximity is a necessary but insufficient starting point, because the placement of children together in the same classroom, dining area or school grounds is not in itself enough to promote social or functional integration. It has often been pointed out, for example, that a pupil who usually works with an assistant in an ordinary classroom may be as segregated from other pupils as one who is withdrawn for special support. Similarly, a pupil who is educated in a separate unit in the school may experience fewer opportunities for integration than one who visits from a special school for regular joint activities. There is a further problem too concerning the implicit hierarchy within Warnock's approach, because it has become apparent that social integration and functional integration must be seen as interconnected. That is, if pupils are to develop positive and sustained relationships with their peers, then this is likely to necessitate their involvement together in well-planned collaborative learning activities.

Hegarty and his colleagues, in their 1981 review of integration schemes across the country, found that many staff held to a view of integration as affecting only that minority of children who would have been segregated in the past. These teachers believed that 'Integration is *their* problem, and success is when they are assimilated into an ordinary school' (Hegarty *et al.* 1981: 15). Such a perspective may also underlie the approach to integration that Jones (1983) described as a 'limpet' model, whereby children are attached as a separate group to a school 'in the hope that some waves of normality will wash over them'. However, dissatisfaction with such narrow interpretations of integration as the 'problem' of the minority, where success is equated to 'fitting a child' into a system which was not designed with his or her needs in mind, has grown. Increasingly, it has been acknowledged that integration must affect all pupils, both those with special educational needs and also their peers. From this perspective, the emphasis is more appropriately placed on the changes that might be necessary in the school as a whole in order to respond to the full range of their needs. The resulting recognition that 'integration is in the end a matter of school reform' (Hegarty 1993: 199) has gathered pace in recent years and has given impetus to a change in terminology away from 'integration' and towards 'inclusion'.

When applied to educational practice in schools, the term inclusion carries with it two main implications: first, that it embraces the needs of all pupils but, second, that for some of them there is a risk of exclusion to be redressed. Thus it refers to the development of a flexible and responsive school system and curriculum which takes as its starting point a recognition of the diversity of pupils' needs (Wedell 1995). However, in addition the term goes well beyond schools, to encompass not only further education and lifelong learning (Tomlinson Committee 1996) but also wider aspects of inclusion within the community.

The different and changing interpretations of what is implied by the terms integration and inclusion inevitably affect attitudes towards inclusive educational provision. From the point of view of both parents and children with special educational needs, inclusive and special school provision offer different possibilities. Concerns about the availability of specialist skills and knowledge in ordinary schools may lead some to express a preference for separate provision. Others, even when they express reservations about the level of support and understanding they will receive from teachers and pupils, prefer the opportunity for access to wider curricular experiences and involvement with local community peer groups that mainstream school can offer. It is clear that their views are likely to be strongly influenced by the quality of their experience of inclusive or separate provision, and the same is undoubtedly true for teachers.

Teachers' attitudes are likely to be influenced by their feelings of confidence about their professional competence to meet special educational needs and by the availability of appropriate support to help them in this task. They are generally reported to be more positive about the inclusion of those with physical or sensory impairments than those with moderate learning difficulties and least positive concerning those with emotional and behavioural difficulties. As Croll and Moses (1985) have pointed out, often teachers may not be fully aware of the educational implications associated with particular physical and sensory impairments, but they are all likely to have had direct experience of the teaching and management challenges that can be posed by significant difficulties in learning and behaviour. These are, however, not only the most frequently occurring forms of special educational need, but also the most complex to define. Factors such as gender, race and home background have all been seen to be involved in the distinctions that are drawn between the level of difficulty that might be met in regular classrooms and that which requires additional or specialist help. It is possible, therefore, that with growing awareness of the interactive and relative nature of their needs, more positive attitudes will develop towards their inclusion.

There is some evidence to support the view that increased knowledge and understanding of special educational needs can lead to different perspectives. For example, a study of the attitudes of teachers who had been trained as special educational needs coordinators (Sugden *et al.* 1989) found that, provided in-service opportunities were made for school staff, the vast majority were in favour of inclusive provision for pupils with moderate learning difficulties. Furthermore, with additional staffing resources, they also supported the education of those with emotional and behavioural difficulties in ordinary schools. By contrast, most of the coordinators felt that the inclusion of pupils with sensory or physical impairments was only appropriate if they were supported by specialist teachers.

Attitudes towards inclusion are likely to be most positive among those teachers who understand the nature of children's difficulties and feel able to draw on their own skills and the support of colleagues to meet a diverse range of needs. Children with special educational needs require an effective means of access to the curriculum, worthwhile and successful learning experiences and a supportive educational environment. These needs will be present for a significant number of pupils in any school. On the whole, it seems reasonable to suppose that those schools that are most successful in meeting existing needs will also respond most positively to the further inclusion of pupils with more specialized needs.

Discussion points

1   In 1981, Hegarty and his colleagues referred to a prevalent view that integration was 'their problem'; that is, the problem of children with special educational needs. To what extent should inclusive education be seen as problematic, and for whom?

2   'Disabilities and difficulties become more or less handicapping depending on the expectations of others and on social contexts' (ILEA 1985). How far would you agree with this proposition? Consider what strategies may be available to teachers in order to ensure that pupils with disabilities are not unnecessarily 'handicapped' in school.

3   The vast majority of special educational needs are identified at school when pupils fail in some way to meet the demands that are made of them. Discuss the role of teacher attitudes and expectations in the identification of learning and emotional or behavioural difficulties.

Further reading

Clark, C., Dyson, A., Millward, A. and Skidmore, D. (1997) *New Directions in Special Needs: Innovations in Mainstream Schools*, London: Cassell.

Thomas, G., Walker, D. and Webb, J. (1998) *The Making of the Inclusive School*, London: Routledge.

Chapter 4

A curriculum for all?

One of the guiding principles underpinning the Code of Practice is that 'children with special educational needs require the greatest possible access to a broad and balanced education, including the National Curriculum' (DfE 1994a: para. 1:2). As this makes clear, the whole curriculum incorporates but goes beyond the National Curriculum. Nevertheless, the introduction of the National Curriculum marked a particularly significant development for special education because it gave, for the first time, a legal entitlement to all children to share in a set of common curricular experiences. In doing so, it required their teachers to be committed to the provision of a curriculum that should be not only broad and balanced, but also 'relevant and differentiated' (NCC 1989b), in order to meet the full range of pupils' needs.

To understand the ways in which this provision has developed, it is helpful to consider the approaches to the curriculum that have influenced special education in the past. Prior to the introduction of the National Curriculum special schools were typically free from some of the constraints, such as external examinations, that applied in mainstream schools. Perhaps as a result, there were many examples of innovative practice in their curriculum development (Farrell 1997). A particular strength was always in the explicit attention paid to aspects of learning that tend to remain part of the 'hidden' curriculum in mainstream education. That is, there was usually an emphasis on planned activities which aim to enhance both feelings of personal worth and also confidence and competence in social interaction. However, the focus tended to be more on the special than on the common educational needs of their pupils, and a risk associated with this was that it could lead to an underestimation of what they might achieve. Such a risk was particularly evident when the curriculum allowed little access to mainstream learning experiences. Overall, though, the most frequently voiced criticism of special school provision at that time concerned the lack of curricular breadth.

By contrast, pupils with special educational needs who attended ordinary schools potentially had access to a wider range of educational opportunities. However, because their needs were rarely seen as a priority for mainstream curriculum design, they were often assigned to a more restricted set of experiences than other pupils in the school, typically with a particular emphasis on basic literacy and numeracy skills. Indeed, it was not unusual in secondary schools in the past for those with learning difficulties to have limited access to specialist subject teachers, and to follow separate syllabuses and specially designed option courses. This gradually began to change as more schools adopted what is often referred to as a 'whole school' approach to special educational provision. The exact form that this takes varies from school to school, but an example from one school is shown in Figure 4.1 on p. 64. As this illustrates, a key principle is that all staff retain responsibility for the education of all pupils.

The introduction of the National Curriculum meant that children with special educational needs in both special and mainstream contexts should have access to a wider range of learning experiences than was previously the case. However, as HMI surveys of the time (1989, 1991) demonstrated, curricular breadth is not enough by itself to ensure that pupils are provided with 'balanced' and 'differentiated' learning experiences. It is, therefore, important to explore what these terms might imply for those with special educational needs.

The Warnock Committee described the aims of education as twofold:

> first, to enlarge a child's knowledge, experience and imaginative understanding, and thus his awareness of moral values and capacity for enjoyment; and secondly, to enable him to enter the world after formal education is over as an active participant in society and a responsible contributor to it, capable of achieving as much independence as possible.
>
> (DES 1978: para. 1.4)

This framework [for a whole school approach] ... assumes that the school AS A WHOLE recognizes the needs of all its pupils and this particularly includes those who may have special educational needs. The whole school is involved in the education and development of these pupils.

It assumes that each pupil will have access to:

(a)   an appropriate curriculum;
(b)   specialist help if this is required;
(c)   an appropriate social and emotional climate;
(d)   counselling and support.

Providing access to an appropriate curriculum is of paramount importance and is the measure by which we could judge our success in providing fully for the educational needs of all our pupils.

Developing positive attitudes towards pupils' needs and their rights to an appropriate education is fundamental if the school is going to develop a truly whole school approach. Similarly, it has to be accepted that the expertise of many people will be needed if pupils' needs are to be met and if appropriate curricula are to be presented.

The basic premise on which we should be working is that no one person should be seen as being responsible for the assessment of needs and neither should one person be responsible for meeting needs. To assess and meet the needs of our pupils demands a coordinated team effort in which each member of the team clearly understands his or her role. It follows on from this that clear role definitions are essential as are clear and well defined lines of communication.

Figure 4.1   Extracts from a secondary school's discussion paper on 'A Whole School Approach to Special Educational Needs'

The question of 'balance' between the individual and social aims of education identified here can be seen as central to curriculum development for all pupils. It becomes a critical consideration for pupils with special educational needs, because for them it also concerns the relative weighting that should appropriately be given to common and more specialized educational aims. Accordingly, it has considerable implications for the time that is made available for sharing the curricular experiences of their peers.

It is important to emphasize that entitlement to a common curriculum does not imply that identical learning activities and teaching approaches will be relevant to the needs of all children. The notion of 'differentiation' refers to the way in which these might be flexibly matched to pupils' experience, skills, knowledge and interests. Alternative models of curriculum development in special education have been concerned with both balance and differentiation. The approaches that have been followed have been influenced not only by the nature of particular needs, however, but also by the way in which these have been conceptualized.

Early approaches to curriculum development in special education

Early approaches to curriculum development were influenced by the view that special educational needs arose primarily from within-child factors. Where children were regarded as simply 'slow', a 'watered-down' and somewhat impoverished version of the mainstream curriculum was generally considered appropriate. Alternatively, when special educational needs were deemed evidence of some specific deficit, there was a view that it might be possible to identify and somehow restore 'the missing skills which … [would] enable them to join the mainstream curriculum again' (Swann 1988b). Thus, for example, it might be the case that pupils were found to have difficulties in tasks which involved auditory or visual discrimination. Where this was so, it was assumed that specific training in these skills would enhance their learning throughout the curriculum. Accordingly, structured programmes were developed whereby pupils were taught to recognize and discriminate between visual or auditory patterns of increasing complexity. The programmes frequently led to improved pupil performance on the set tasks. Not surprisingly, however, when these skills were taught in isolation they were rarely found to transfer to other areas of learning. Increasingly, therefore, doubts were raised about the validity of trying to isolate and 'treat' apparent problems in this way. As a result, the effectiveness of the approach, as well as its relevance to the curriculum as a whole, was brought into question.

This is not to suggest that methods that focus on perceived within-child deficits no longer exist. For example, in those cases where pupils have specific impairments which impede their learning, it may well be thought appropriate to incorporate special aims into their general curricular experiences. Nevertheless, by the late 1970s, dissatisfaction had grown with what could generally be achieved by a curriculum which was centred on a deficit interpretation of learning difficulties. Accordingly, behavioural perspectives began to dominate the curriculum design and teaching methods of special education.

A behavioural objectives approach

This approach does not emphasize the within-child factors that might contribute to learning difficulty. Instead, it directs attention towards an analysis of the skills that children need in order to learn specific tasks, and the sequence in which these might be acquired. From a behavioural perspective, all behaviour is learned in ways which are governed by both the setting in which it arises and also by the consequences that follow. The evidence that learning has occurred takes the form of a change in observable behaviour. Thus, the focus is placed on what learners demonstrate that they can do after learning, and no attempt is made to interpret their inner experiences or cognitive strategies. When applied to curriculum design, the behavioural approach draws on Tyler's (1949) principle that the objectives or intended learning outcomes of teaching should be defined with sufficient clarity that teachers can assess through direct observation whether or not they have been met.

Solity and Bull (1987) have described the stages involved in curriculum development when it is based on a behavioural model. First, selected subject areas are broken down into units of study: in one of their examples, for instance, mathematics might incorporate units dealing with the language of instruction, problem-solving, money, time, addition, subtraction, and so on. Then the goal of each unit of study is identified and expressed in behavioural terms; that is, as a precise statement of what a pupil will do in order to demonstrate that a skill has been learned. These statements are referred to as behavioural objectives, and are characterized by:

(i) the use of observable verbs, such as 'write', 'select' and 'name', rather than non-observable verbs, such as 'know', 'understand' or 'appreciate';
(ii) a description of the conditions in which the pupil will demonstrate the skill, such as 'when presented with two sets of objects' or 'within ten minutes'; and
(iii) a specification of the criteria upon which his or her performance will be judged to be successful, such as 'to within two millimetres of accuracy on nine out of ten occasions'.

Thus, for example, the goal of one unit in geography might be described as 'locating and identifying features on a map'. Translated into a behavioural objective, this could become:

Given an OS map at a scale of 1:50,000, the pupil will:
(i) locate on the map the points identified by five grid references; (ii) name the features represented by the symbols at those points on three consecutive occasions with 100 per cent accuracy.

The next stage is to analyse the component skills that are necessary in order to attain each objective, again expressing them in behavioural terms. These components should then be sequenced into steps through which the pupil can progress towards achieving the objective. A number of examples of such skills analyses have been published for use by schools (e.g. Ainscow and Tweddle 1979, 1984), and some LEAs have adapted and developed these further. The approach relies heavily on the view that, by comparison with others, children with learning difficulties need more structured and detailed planning of the curricular opportunities that are made available to them, and benefit from clearly expressed and finely graded steps in their learning. As a general rule, the more extensive a pupil's learning difficulties, the smaller each step in the sequence will be.

It can be seen that the behavioural objectives approach focuses on what pupils will do as a result of their learning. It emphasizes detailed planning in which intended learning outcomes are clearly specified in advance. Accordingly, it has widely been acknowledged to promote precise and purposeful curriculum design. A particular strength is in the basis it provides for continuous monitoring and evaluation of a pupil's progress towards the stated objectives. Furthermore, it implies a positive view of pupil learning, because any lack of progress is not attributed to fixed or inherent learner characteristics, but rather to the need to revise and modify some aspect of the curriculum in order to ensure that difficulties are overcome. Considerable success has been reported in the use of a behaviourally-based curriculum for the teaching of basic skills, such as literacy and numeracy, to pupils with a wide range of special educational needs. Moreover, the clarity with which objectives are formulated allows for easy communication between teachers and colleagues, parents and the pupils themselves about expectations, progress and attainment.

However, a number of criticisms have been raised about the approach. There is no doubt that behavioural objectives are easier to determine in some areas of the curriculum than others. Specifically, they are most readily applied to 'skills' rather than to aspects of knowledge and understanding. Furthermore, they may only be relevant to certain forms of learning, because it is not always possible or desirable to specify the exact nature of the intended outcomes in advance. The attempt to do so can constrain the opportunities for more open-ended learning activities, in which pupils are encouraged to develop their own problem-solving strategies. A narrow focus on the 'products' of learning can serve to distract attention from the processes that are involved, and this in turn may lead to pupils being viewed as passive recipients of teaching rather than as active participants in the learning process. Thus, as Barnes (1982) has argued, while specific behavioural objectives play an important role in curriculum planning, they represent a 'bad fit' in those aspects where the pupils' own contribution to their learning is of particular significance.

It has generally been acknowledged, therefore, even by some of those who initially espoused the approach (e.g. Ainscow and Tweddle 1988), that where behavioural principles are the sole influence on curriculum development, this is likely to lead to a restricted and arid range of learning opportunities, in which the acquisition of basic skills is given an inappropriate priority over other equally important areas of experience. As a result of these concerns, there has been a move in special education towards what Brennan (1985) has described as an 'extended objectives' approach.

An extended objectives approach

An extended objectives approach seeks to balance the rigour in planning and effectiveness in teaching specified skills that is associated with behavioural perspectives with an equally explicit focus on the opportunities that are provided for self-expression, problem-solving and self-directed learning. That is, it aims to address the question not only of what pupils are to do as a result of their learning, but also of the processes by which they are to be actively involved in extending their knowledge, skills and understanding. This implies that curriculum planning must focus on the strategies that teachers use to promote learning, as well as on the content of what they teach.

An emphasis on the processes of learning is associated with the work of Stenhouse (1975). He stressed that learning activities should be designed which were of intrinsic value to pupils, rather than simply the means to achieve predetermined ends. Accordingly, these should be planned in such a way that pupils at different levels of understanding would be able to experience success. Some have argued that his 'process model' lends itself to a more flexible curriculum design for those with special educational needs than the behavioural objectives approach (Goddard 1983; Thomas and Feiler 1988). That is, a greater responsiveness to the full range of pupils' needs may be possible where the emphasis is placed on individual aims and goals rather than on set criteria of success and failure in meeting fixed objectives.

This may well be so. However, the more that outcomes are seen to be open-ended and sometimes unpredictable, the greater the difficulty for a teacher in assessing what pupils have taken from their curricular experiences, and therefore in planning for continuity and progression in their learning. This is necessary for all pupils, and it can be argued that it is even more important where their rate of progress is uneven or slow. It has been increasingly accepted, therefore, that what is required in curriculum planning is a balanced combination of behavioural objectives together with others which are equally carefully structured, but which provide more flexible opportunities for the development of problem-solving and self-expression in pupils' learning. Through this means, explicit attention can be given to social, emotional and cognitive processes in learning, as well as to the more overt signs of achievement.

Wider perspectives

The discussion so far has centred on formal aspects of curriculum design, but it should be acknowledged that the relationship between the learning opportunities that are planned and intended and the actual experiences of individual pupils is a complex one. An 'ecological' perspective on children's development and learning emphasizes the ways in which individuals both influence and are influenced by the different learning environments that they experience, and by the relationships between these. Such a perspective has significant implications for curriculum development, for it highlights the importance for pupils' progress of the relationships that exist, not only between the learning contexts of home, school and community, but also within the school itself (Thomas and Feiler 1988). Thus the effects of school organization, pupil groupings and the quality of staff, pupil and staff–pupil relationships on the way in which the curriculum is experienced should all be taken into account. From this standpoint, it can be argued that it may be through adaptations to the climate for learning, as much as through modifications of specific tasks and activities, that the curricular needs of pupils with special educational needs may best be met.

Balance and differentiation in the curriculum

The different approaches to curriculum development that have been outlined here can be seen to vary in the emphasis they give to special educational aims, precisely defined learning outcomes, processes and the context of relationships within which learning takes place. It seems reasonable to suppose that a balanced curriculum should incorporate explicit attention to all these aspects, for it is unlikely that any one approach could meet all the needs of pupils with learning difficulties. Where special educational aims associated with specific impairments to learning are required they should be integrated as fully as possible within the general framework of the common curriculum. The appropriate balance between specialized and 'normal' curricular experiences may vary for different pupils, but the principle of maximum possible access to the mainstream curriculum should apply. It is important to remember though that, on the whole, the better the quality of the curriculum for all pupils, the less likely it is that many additional or alternative aims will be required. However, it is widely accepted that pupils who experience learning difficulties will need more time than their peers if they are to achieve success in some areas of their learning, and this has implications for the priority that is allocated to these areas within the curriculum.

Literacy and numeracy skills are highly valued in our society and therefore it is not surprising that, prior to the introduction of the National Curriculum, many schools restricted the breadth of the curriculum that was made available to pupils with learning difficulties in order to concentrate attention on the teaching of these skills. However, while it was an understandable response to the practical problems of time management that are associated with meeting special educational needs, it could result in regrettable consequences. For example, a narrow focus on areas of difficulty can often lead to both boredom and frustration. It can also result in a lowering of morale, because fewer opportunities are made available in which pupils might develop areas of relative strength. These issues have recently been highlighted again, in particular for primary teachers, by the introduction of the national literacy strategy (DfEE 1998b) and the forthcoming national numeracy strategy.

There is, then, a dilemma for teachers in the balance they seek between acknowledging and responding to pupils' special educational needs while at the same time trying to ensure that they have access to the full range of curricular experiences. Brennan (1985) has proposed that one way forward is to distinguish between different forms of learning within the curriculum, which he characterizes as 'functional' and 'contextual'. He describes functional learning as that which is judged essential for a pupil: as such, it must be accurate, permanent, thorough and proficient. By contrast, contextual learning allows a pupil to relate to the 'natural, social, emotional and aesthetic' aspects of his or her environment. Thus it involves awareness, familiarity, recognition and appreciation. At first glance, this may simply appear to represent a more sophisticated gloss on the traditional dichotomy between 'the basics' and other aspects of the curriculum. However, Brennan argues that functional and contextual learning should be viewed as interactive and complementary elements of a pupil's learning experience. That is, the skills and knowledge acquired in the former should be drawn upon in more open-ended and self-expressive activities. These, because of their emphasis on achievements of personal relevance to the pupil, may in turn give more sense of purpose and motivation to functional learning. The balance between functional and contextual learning will vary from pupil to pupil and over time, according to needs and progress, but a central principle here is that the more restricted a pupil's achievements in functional areas of learning, the broader and more important the contextual aspects must become. It may be seen, therefore, that Brennan is advocating a rather different balance of curricular experiences from that which has traditionally been provided. Furthermore, his perspective demonstrates that the notion of balance in the curriculum is intimately bound up with the concept of differentiation.

The consideration of differentiation is not unique to pupils with special educational needs, for it concerns the means by which the curriculum can be adapted in such a way that learning activities are made meaningful and relevant to all pupils, and offer each the opportunity to experience success. Thus it can be seen to be central to effective teaching. Where the curriculum has been designed to meet the full range of pupils' needs as far as possible, then fewer adaptations will be required for individuals or groups, but at the same time any that are necessary should be easier to accommodate. It is implicit within the concept of special educational need, however, that some pupils require additional help if they are to benefit fully from the learning opportunities that are generally provided. Furthermore, those with the most extensive difficulties will require the greatest attention to flexible adaptations to objectives, teaching approaches and organizational arrangements. It is, therefore, possible to describe a continuum of increasingly differentiated curricular provision which parallels the continuum of special educational need.

Common curriculum with additional support as needed

In its early guidance to schools concerning the curriculum for children with special educational needs, the National Curriculum Council noted that:

> schools that successfully meet the demands of a diverse range of individual needs through agreed policies on teaching and learning approaches are invariably effective in meeting special educational needs.
>
> (NCC 1989a: para. 5)

If there is flexibility in the pace at which pupils are required to learn, and if work is matched to variation in learning styles, interests, experience and attainment, then the majority of those with special educational needs are not likely to require further differentiation of the curriculum.

To this end, the National Curriculum Council stressed that schools should draw up their curriculum plans in such a way as to ensure that curricular breadth is accessible to all pupils and, furthermore, that a consideration of special educational needs should be integral to the design of the schemes of work that form the core of the curriculum. In implementing these, explicit attention should be given to the balance between individualized and group work, to flexible pupil groupings and to a varied range of teaching methods and materials. Full use should also be made of whatever support is available from parents, colleagues and other professionals. A basic principle put forward is 'for access to the curriculum to be facilitated by whatever means necessary to ensure that success is achieved' (NCC 1989a: para. 6). For some pupils, this will involve the provision of additional support in the form of special aids and equipment, and others may require supplementary teaching assistance on an individual or small group basis. Where the common curriculum has been designed with all the pupils in mind, however, further differentiation should only be necessary for the minority whose needs cannot fully be met through these means.

Common curriculum with partial modification

For those pupils with specific impairments that impede or restrict their access to general learning opportunities, additional educational aims may necessarily be incorporated into their curriculum. For example, blind children will need teaching in the use of Braille and other tactile aids to their learning, and those with significant language difficulties are likely to need specific programmes to develop their functional communication skills. When this is the case, decisions must be made about the relative priority of special and common educational aims, because time spent on the former inevitably has implications across the rest of the curriculum. As far as possible, the attempt should be made to integrate special aims into mainstream learning experiences, but if specialized needs are to be met effectively, then this is likely to involve some modification or reduction in the rest of the pupil's curriculum. Here, the question of relevance is often raised. For example, how relevant is it to a pupil with physical impairment to be included in P.E. lessons? How relevant is it for a blind pupil to have access to the visual arts programme or for a pupil with specific language difficulties to have the opportunity to learn French? Such questions are not as easily answered as some have suggested, and require collaborative decision-making and continuous reassessment and review. With good reason it can be argued that no area of the curriculum should automatically be regarded as being of little relevance to a pupil with particular special educational needs.

Far more frequent than the addition to or modification of educational aims in order to meet special educational needs, however, are modifications to the ways in which pupils are helped to access the curriculum. These may include the sorts of adaptation to curricular tasks and activities, teaching methods and organizational strategies that are addressed in the following chapter. Whatever form they take, the underlying aim must be to build on pupils' strengths, as well as help overcome areas of difficulty.

Modified common curriculum

Where pupils' learning difficulties extend across most areas of the curriculum, they are likely to require even more explicit attention to the ways in which their needs can be met, while at the same time ensuring that they maintain as much common ground with their peers as possible. This will include, for example, careful consideration of the level at which tasks are set, the presentation and balance of activities, and the degree and style of assistance that will best facilitate their learning and thus ensure progress.

Wholly or partly special curriculum

Finally, in those cases where individual needs are such that it is judged that special goals should take priority in a child's education, then a wholly or partly alternative curriculum may be provided. It should be emphasized, however, that if it is accepted that the general aims of education are the same for all children (DES 1978; NCC 1989b), then it follows that any necessary alternatives should be developed in ways which are consistent with this principle.

The National Curriculum for children with special educational needs

As discussed in Chapter 2, many commentators have pointed out that children with special educational needs were not explicitly considered when the framework for the National Curriculum was first drawn up. Indeed, at one point it was intended that those with statements of special educational need would automatically be excluded from its provisions. However, it was acknowledged that such exclusion would be in direct contradiction to the principles of greater inclusion that had been increasingly accepted since the publication of the Warnock Report.

Despite the lack of specific attention to their needs, in many ways the National Curriculum represented a significant step forward for those with learning difficulties, because their entitlement to a common curriculum with their peers served to emphasize the continuum between 'special' and 'ordinary' educational provision. Other positive features, in addition to its breadth, are its emphasis on detailed planning and monitoring of progress. A whole school approach to planning programmes of study can do much to promote the view that all staff share responsibility for the educational progress of all their pupils. Furthermore, a school-wide approach to continuous assessment together with a detailed system of record-keeping, which is shared with both pupils and their parents, can serve to heighten awareness of and responsiveness to individual needs. There has been a commitment in schools to make the National Curriculum accessible for children with the full range of special educational needs and, in practice, very few children have been exempted from its provisions.

From her national survey of mainstream primary teachers following implementation of the National Curriculum, Lewis (1995a) found that they reported a wide range of benefits for children with special educational needs. Their comments included reference to the way in which it provided a basic educational entitlement, together with a clear curricular framework and structure for the differentiation of learning experiences. HMI, reporting on the impact of the National Curriculum (1990, 1991), also described positive effects on teacher expectations and the quality of their assessment and record-keeping. This does not imply, however, that there were no problems in its implementation. Although the HMI reports commented favourably on the breadth of the curricular experiences which were offered, it is understandable that some teachers felt under pressure to give most time and attention to those subjects that were to be formally assessed, at the expense of a more balanced approach to the curriculum. In addition, the timetabling constraints of the statutory subject-based programmes of study posed difficulties for teachers in two main areas of particular importance for children with special educational needs: that is, in the provision of sufficient opportunities for consolidating learning, and also in giving proper attention to personal and social aspects of education.

Revisions to the National Curriculum were introduced in 1995 which offered greater flexibility for schools to meet a wider range of their pupils' needs (DfE 1995). In particular, schools welcomed the overall reduction in specified curriculum content, which allowed more time to be given to other curriculum activities. Other changes of particular relevance for children with special educational needs included: first, the explicit acknowledgement that forms of communication other than written language could be used to access the curriculum; and second, greater freedom for children to work on the material from Programmes of Study most appropriate for their levels of achievement, rather than only on that which is identified for their age group. Lewis, writing at the time, predicted that because such increased flexibility made the National Curriculum more inclusive, then this might potentially reduce the proportion of children identified as in need of statements (Lewis 1995b). That this did not happen is perhaps in part related to the impact of the Code of Practice. In principle, the National Curriculum provides a coherent structure within which the Code's progressive differentiation strategies and identification of educational priorities fit quite well. However, by strengthening the school-based procedures and responsibilities for children with special educational needs the Code also served to raise their profile in schools. This, taken together with the continuing emphasis on comparing schools' academic performance through published league tables, is likely to have contributed to the pressure towards increased rather than reduced referrals for statements.

Continuing curriculum developments

The introduction of the national literacy strategy (DfEE 1998b) and forthcoming numeracy strategy in primary schools has reasserted and reinforced the importance within the curriculum of literacy and numeracy skills. Many children with special educational needs experience difficulties in the development of these skills, which frequently feature on their Individual Education Plans (IEPs). DfEE guidance makes it clear that all children are to be included in the daily literacy hour with their peers unless there are convincing reasons why they should be withdrawn, and the same is likely to be true in relation to numeracy. In both cases, an emphasis is placed on whole class teaching, which has caused concerns about the extent to which children with special educational needs will be able to keep up with the pace, and the sort of additional support required to help them benefit. However, the evidence from schools which took part in piloting the literacy strategy is that children with special educational needs have made more progress than was anticipated as a result of their involvement (Anwyll 1998). Attention has been drawn to the opportunities the literacy hour offers to promote inclusion, increase the amount of time that children are exposed to print, provide positive models and foster both peer collaboration and also greater independence (Moss and Reason 1998; Reason 1998). Nevertheless, it is clear that it also poses considerable organizational and teaching challenges. IEP targets will need to be incorporated in the group and individual components of the literacy hour, but the DfEE acknowledges that they may also need to be worked on at additional times. This puts great pressure both on the provision of IEP priorities in other areas of learning and also on the timetabling of broader curricular activities. It is essential, therefore, that the impact on the breadth and balance of children's learning experiences is monitored and evaluated.

Curricular issues are central in special education for when the curriculum is not planned in such a way as to be responsive to individual variation, then learning difficulties will almost inevitably result. For this reason, writers such as Swann (1988b) have warned that 'access' to the curriculum is not necessarily a helpful way of looking at children's needs; rather, it may be that the curriculum itself is in need of change. The main frameworks by which schools must plan and develop the curriculum are defined by the National Curriculum and ongoing government initiatives such as those in literacy and numeracy. The challenge for teachers is to try to ensure that the entitlement to participation in these initiatives results in positive learning experiences for all their pupils, including those with special educational needs.

Discussion points

1   How far can and should the consideration of individual needs take priority over common needs in curriculum planning? What dilemmas are involved in meeting pupils' special needs while at the same time ensuring that they have the opportunity to participate in the full range of curricular activities available to their peers?

2   'Behavioural objectives are easier to determine in some areas of the curriculum than others.' Consider which areas of the

curriculum these might be, and discuss the main strengths and limitations of the approach.

3   What would you see as the most important issues for teachers if they are to ensure that pupils with special educational needs benefit from their involvement in the national literacy and numeracy strategies?

Further reading

Brennan, W. K. (1985) *Curriculum for Special Needs*, Milton Keynes: Open University Press.

Lewis, A. (1995) *Primary Special Needs and the National Curriculum*, 2nd edn, London: Routledge.

Chapter 5

Teaching approaches and organizational strategies

Within any class group there is considerable variation between pupils in their style and rate of learning, and in their educational attainments. If learning activities are to be made meaningful, relevant and attainable for all pupils, then it is central to a teacher's task to find ways to respond to that diversity, and this is true whether or not some of the pupils are judged to have special educational needs. The more extensive a particular pupil's learning difficulties, the more apparent will be the need for carefully planned adaptations to the general teaching approach. However, the principles that underlie these adaptations are the same across the full range of individual pupil variation. That is, while it should not be denied that specialist methods may be required for those with specific impairments, it is important to emphasize that, on the whole, children with special educational needs learn from teaching approaches which are also effective for their peers. Thus it is difficult to make a qualitative distinction between 'special' and 'ordinary' practice. Rather, it can be argued that where children have special educational needs, this requires us to look more closely at those factors that we understand to promote effective learning for all children: from this perspective, the needs of children with learning difficulties are for 'good' educational practice.

Classroom-based assessment

Pupils with special educational needs show as great a range of individual variation as their peers, and accordingly individual classroom-based assessment must be the starting point for deter-mining the type and degree of assistance that will help them in their learning. The importance of identifying relative strengths as well as weaknesses in this process cannot be overstated, as the aim must be both to build on existing strengths and to overcome areas of diffi-culty. Furthermore, because special educational needs are interactive in nature, it is essential that teachers gather information about how pupils' strengths and weaknesses interact with the learning demands of the classroom. An individual pupil's approach to learning will vary in the contexts of different tasks and activities, organizational strategies, teaching methods and classroom relation-ships. The aim of classroom-based assessment, therefore, must be to attempt to analyse the ways in which a pupil's skills, knowledge and understanding interact with these aspects of the classroom environment (Norwich 1990).

Such an assessment involves both direct observation and also individual discussion with the pupils. It is useful first to gather general observational evidence of their responses to classroom routines, tasks and relationships. Particular concerns here might include the degree to which they demonstrate initiative and self-management in their learning; for example, by organizing their own materials, maintaining attention to tasks, and knowing when and how to seek help (Westwood 1997). Teachers sometimes find it helpful to adopt checklists of questions in order to structure their observations. For example, Figure 5.1 overleaf shows part of a pupil behaviour checklist which was drawn up by a special educational needs coordinator (SENCO) in a comprehensive school to help his colleagues be more precise in their observations of individual pupils' learning behaviour.

Comparisons of the observations made of individual pupils in different classroom activities should reveal any variations in their approach to learning which are associated with particular sorts of task demands and learning contexts. From these initial observations it can also often be the case that questions arise which merit more systematic investigation. These might include, for example, how often a pupil seeks teacher reassurance during lessons or how much of the allocated time a pupil actually spends engaged with a set task, and whether this differs according to the type of activity or

Does the pupil:

1   Accept familiar tasks willingly?
2   Accept unfamiliar tasks willingly?
3   Start tasks immediately?
4   Ask for help if appropriate?
5   Only begin tasks if understands?
6   Show motivation to complete tasks?
7   Resist distractions?
8   Cope with task frustrations?
9   Complete tasks in given time?

Figure 5.1 An extract from a comprehensive school's screening checklist for pupils' task-related behaviour

pupil grouping. The answers to questions of this kind can alert teachers to factors that appear to contribute to a pupil's difficulty.

If pupils are to be helped to achieve progress and success in their learning, then this necessitates close monitoring of their level of grasp of the skills, knowledge and concepts required by specific curricular tasks. Observations of their general approach to learning must therefore be complemented by more focused curriculum-based assessment. This should involve not only an evaluation of the work produced, but also direct observations of the way in which the pupils engage with the task. It is equally important to listen to what the pupils have to say about their work. For those experiencing difficulties, it is valuable to compare what can be done independently with what can be done when provided with varying degrees of help. Through individual discussion, teachers can try to find out the pupils' own perceptions of the purpose of the task and their explanations of the strategies they used in carrying it out. Hart (1996) emphasizes the need to try to look at classroom activities from the pupils' point of view, and be prepared to reflect on a range of possible explanations for the difficulties they experience. Lewis (1995b) suggests that, both in their observations and discussions, key concerns for teachers must include the extent to which pupils understand what they have been asked to do, the nature of any consistent error patterns in their work, and how successfully they have retained and used earlier learning in their approach to the task.

It should be apparent that the assessment process outlined above is not confined to children with special educational needs. However, the Code of Practice (DfE 1994a) makes it clear that it is essential for those experiencing difficulties in their learning. There is no doubt that regular and detailed observational assessment of this kind is time-consuming. If it is to be valuable to both teachers and pupils, therefore, it should help inform planning for teaching. That is, the evidence gathered should enable teachers:

(i)   to determine priorities and starting points for learning;
(ii) to form hypotheses about factors in the interaction between pupil and learning environment which assist or hinder progress; and
(iii) to identify the sorts of flexible adaptation that might best help the pupil to achieve success.

Once these adaptations have been introduced, then continuous assessment and detailed record-keeping of pupil progress should allow their effectiveness to be monitored and reviewed. The approach is therefore fundamental to the continuing cycle of assessment, planning, action and review which is outlined in the Code.

The Code is also explicit about the need to involve both pupils and parents in the process. It points out that children not only have a right to be involved, but also have a significant contribution to make. They may, for example, have their own insights into the sorts of assistance that would help them to overcome particular difficulties. Furthermore, there has been an increasing recognition of the importance of involving them as fully as possible in self-evaluation and monitoring of their own progress. Wolfendale (1987) has argued that teachers have a responsibility to help all children to:

understand the point and purpose of the learning tasks presented to them and in which they engage;

learn how to learn;
evolve effective learning strategies;
identify learning hurdles, 'sticking points' along the way, and
apply appropriate problem-solving learning strategies.

(ibid.: 37)

Such a perspective highlights the need to foster children's active involvement in and reflection on their own learning, including the assessment of their strengths, weaknesses, achievements and learning needs. Children with learning difficulties can too easily become passive learners in the classroom who neither expect nor are expected to initiate ideas and activities. Yet it is reasonable to suppose that they may engage with their learning more actively and with a greater sense of purpose if they are enabled to: see clearly what they are aiming for and why; recognize how this builds upon and takes further their existing knowledge, skills and experience; and, with support, monitor their own progress through the various steps towards achieving their learning goals.

Partnership with parents is described as one of the 'fundamental principles' of the Code of Practice. Parents have an in-depth knowledge and experience of their own children that can only add to teachers' understanding of their needs. They represent a unique source of information about their child's interests, learning experiences and social interactions, both at home and in other out-of-school contexts. They can also have important insights to offer about their child's response to school, and about the type of strategies that might be most effective in overcoming areas of difficulty. Significantly, these strategies may involve closer home–school cooperation and a joint approach to facilitating their child's learning, for there is no doubt that where parents and teachers work together collaboratively, this is to the benefit of the children concerned.

For a more complete assessment profile of a pupil, of course, classroom-based assessment will also need to be complemented by information from other sources, including other school staff and, where appropriate, support agencies from educational and other services. The support that a class teacher may draw on from parents and from colleagues and other professionals, is discussed more fully in Chapter 7.

The formulation of individual education plans (IEPs)

The quality of the plans that teachers develop to promote children's learning is dependent on the quality of the assessment information that they gather. Where an Individual Educational Plan (IEP) is to be drawn up, the Code of Practice (DfE 1994a) specifies that this should include attention to: the nature of the child's learning difficulties; the action to be taken, including specific targets for intervention; and procedures for monitoring, evaluation and review. As discussed above, it is also important that plans are based on a recognition of strengths as well as weaknesses and incorporate both child and parent perspectives. At the same time, to be practicable, they need to be framed concisely. A number of examples of IEP proformas and questions to help parents prepare for reviews have been published (e.g. Hornby *et al.* 1995; DfEE 1997b), and many LEAs also provide their own versions for schools. Teachers need to be aware of the concerns that have been expressed that IEPs may too readily focus on within-child deficits and narrowly defined behavioural objectives, and serve to isolate individual children (Goddard 1997). As Hart (1998) has demonstrated though, this need not be the case: IEPs can be drawn up in a way that emphasizes the interactive nature of children's learning, and the action to be taken should be sensitively incorporated wherever possible into ongoing work with peers. The planned intervention is likely to involve adaptations to curricular tasks and activities, to teaching methods and/or to organizational arrangements.

Adaptations to curricular tasks and activities

A major concern in the planning of curricular tasks and activities is that these should be sufficiently well matched to pupils' existing learning so as to ensure continuity and progression. This implies that planning should take account of diversity in both pace and level of learning. Children with special educational needs are almost invariably described as slow to complete certain types of set work and, therefore, if they are to experience the sense of achievement that derives from the satisfactory completion of a varied and balanced range of curricular activities, this has implications for the design of tasks which can realistically be undertaken in the time that is allocated.

Pace of learning is, of course, partly associated with the provision of realistic learning demands. Some children may experience difficulty in perceiving what is required of them, and in understanding what strategies they need to apply. Accordingly, they can appear to be distracted by irrelevant aspects of the activity, and adopt what to an outsider may seem an unsystematic approach to the task. Difficulties are particularly likely to arise in those tasks that involve abstract or complex ideas, where the step between their existing learning and what is required may simply be too large to take without additional assistance.

It is important, therefore, that in their planning teachers attempt to analyse quite explicitly the skills, knowledge and problem-solving strategies involved in particular tasks, and that they use their curriculum-based assessments to identify what, if any, gaps in learning or other hurdles pupils will need help to overcome. Where their existing levels of learning are such that the task demands are too great, pupils are likely to benefit from a more structured set of activities designed to enable them to progress step by step towards their curriculum goals. The size of each step or 'intermediate goal' (NCC 1989b) should be carefully matched so that it is within pupils' reach but is sufficiently stretching to challenge and motivate them.

In some cases the setting of intermediate goals can be informed by the sort of task analysis associated with an objectives-based approach to the curriculum described in the previous chapter. This involves an attempt to specify and sequence the skills and knowledge a pupil needs in order to achieve the longer-term curriculum goal, and to use the resulting analysis as a basis for developing a set of activities through which they can be taught. However, task analysis has its limitations: it is more readily applied to some areas of the curriculum than others and, even where it is possible to describe a 'logical' sequence of steps, it should be borne in mind that pupils learn by different routes. Accordingly, it is rarely possible to specify in advance a single 'correct' progression that will be effective for all learners. Nevertheless, the underlying principles can be used with some flexibility, and the attempt to analyse a specific task as precisely as possible is a valuable aid to more structured curriculum planning.

In addition to the structuring of curricular tasks, attention in planning may also need to be given to the opportunities that are provided for pupils to practise and consolidate recently developed learning. Pupils with learning difficulties are often characterized as having a poor memory for newly acquired knowledge and skills, and where this is so they will need curricular experiences which allow them actively to rehearse these. To be effective in helping them consolidate their learning, though, it is not sufficient to require pupils to continue to repeat the same inaccurately completed exercise until they 'get it right'. Rather, activities will be needed which enable them to review previous learning in a range of purposeful and interesting contexts.

Furthermore, if pupils are to make the best functional use of the knowledge, skills and learning strategies that they have acquired, they need to recognize how these can be generalized and applied in adaptable ways to novel learning situations. Thus, for example, in the early stages of their mathematical learning they will need to learn that the same strategies are involved in counting or in adding regardless of the materials (e.g. bricks, books, sweets, people) that are to be used. Later, they will need to learn that they can apply computational strategies flexibly to problems such as: $5 + 3 = ?$; $5 + ? = 8$; or 'I should have eight felt tip pens, but I can only find five ...'; and so on. The ease with which learners are able to make such generalizations, and the flexibility with which they adapt to novel problem-solving tasks, will partly depend on how complete a grasp they have of the necessary strategies as well as on how confident they feel using them. However, it is important for teachers to be aware that many pupils with learning difficulties appear to need help in applying their skills to new learning contexts. It will be necessary, therefore, to plan specific activities that will facilitate this.

It can be seen, then, that in order to meet the full range of pupils' needs, adaptations may be required in the pacing and structure of intermediate goals, the provision of additional consolidation activities and the degree of explicit planning to promote generalization. Where children find a learning activity particularly difficult, it can make a great deal of difference to their effort and motivation if tasks can be tailored to their interests. They are also likely to engage with tasks more readily if they can participate in a 'hands-on' fashion. A guiding principle in planning, therefore, must be to provide the sort of practical and active tasks that build on their strengths, interests and first-hand experiences. Any necessary differentiation to tasks and activities must be planned with sensitivity in order to ensure that the work is not seen as unchallenging and of low status, and that pupils do not feel singled out as different and separate from others in the class. Furthermore, it is important to emphasize that no matter how much structured help and guidance they may require on certain tasks, they also need the same range and variety in their curricular experiences – including opportunities for open-ended learning, choice and self-direction – as their peers.

Teaching methods

From the preceding discussion it should be clear that while adaptations to curricular tasks and activities can have a very important role to play in helping pupils overcome learning difficulties, they represent only one aspect of the planning that may be necessary in order to meet the full range of individual educational needs. In this section, attention is drawn to some of the teaching methods that can be employed to support pupils' learning.

It can be argued that the preparation of materials to support pupils' learning is a particularly significant aspect of the teacher's role in responding to special educational needs. Furthermore, it entails the sort of advanced planning that can only be of benefit to all pupils (Hodgson 1989). Few pupils will require specialized aids or equipment in their learning, but where, for example, a visually impaired pupil requires material to be produced in enlarged print, Braille or on tape, then this clearly necessitates making arrangements well in advance. More generally, though, it is important to recognize that an over-reliance on written material is likely to put many children with learning difficulties at a disadvantage, and therefore other media, such as visual, auditory or tactile aids, should be incorporated where possible. As highlighted in a recent government Green Paper (DfEE 1997a), developments in ICT have opened up significant educational opportunities for those with special educational needs. These opportunities do not only include enhanced access to the curriculum for children with sensory, physical and communication difficulties, but also assisted learning for children with a wide range of needs. For example, concept keyboards and CD-ROM offer access for children with literacy difficulties and word-processing programs can support the development of their writing skills. Software programs, such as for arithmetic and spelling, allow children to practise basic skills and consolidate their learning, while more open-ended problem-solving functions can be addressed through the use of databases, control and adventure programs and simulations (Hawkridge and Vincent 1992).

Although children with special educational needs can be significantly supported by the use of a wide range of media, it must be acknowledged that written materials remain central to a great deal of teaching. Published worksheets and textbooks often require some modification if they are not to present an unnecessary hurdle to their learning. Whether adapting such written material or producing their own, teachers need to give attention to vocabulary, sentence length and reading level, as well as to the clarity with which information or instructions are sequenced. Print size, page layout and the use of cues to help focus and direct a pupil's reading may be further considerations (see, for example, Lewis 1995b), and ICT offers teachers a powerful tool for making these sorts of adaptations for children with special educational needs. Whatever form written materials take, however, it is important to ensure that they are complemented by the provision of a variety of 'concrete' examples with which pupils can actively engage and derive first-hand practical experience.

The process of preparing materials frequently involves some decisions about the sort of response that will be expected from pupils, and, while certain curricular tasks clearly require a written form of response, others do not. Those children who have difficulty in writing may engage with tasks more enthusiastically and also reveal a great deal more about what they have learned from their activities where they can present this, at least initially, in other ways. These might include, for example, spoken discussion, drawing, role play or practical demonstration, and it should be noted that aspects of the National Curriculum assessment do allow for such alternative forms of response for particular pupils with special educational needs.

Teacher language and teacher–pupil interaction are fundamental to the teaching-learning process, and there is no doubt that the clarity with which teachers introduce and present tasks has a significant influence on their pupils' learning. Ainscow (1989) has suggested that most children who 'don't get on' in lessons appear unaware or uncertain of what it is they are meant to do and why. In order to ensure that all pupils have a clear understanding of the purpose of the learning activities with which they are to engage, it is self-evident that instructions and explanations should be explicit and unambiguous. Thus teachers need to monitor the language structures and vocabulary that they use, and to modify these according to pupils' responses. It is equally important that they discuss and check pupils' understanding of the strategies that they need to employ, both before they begin and also once they are working on the task. Attention will therefore need to be given to the sorts of questioning technique that may best elicit information from the pupils concerning their grasp of the task in hand.

The aim of teacher talk should not only be to check on pupils' understanding but also to 'extend and explore' their knowledge, to encourage them to make connections between different elements and to model problem-solving and reflection (Watson 1996). This requires close monitoring of children's engagement with learning activities and responsive feedback on how they are progressing. Regular feedback has a significant role in supporting children who are experiencing learning difficulties. Through corrective feedback teachers can help to prevent the development of persistent errors or misconceptions, and through positive feedback they can offer encouragement and reassurance. To be effective in extending learning, their positive feedback should be sufficiently explicit and specific that it helps pupils to see exactly how and why their learning strategies have been successful. Teacher praise is important for all pupils and perhaps particularly so for those with learning difficulties, for it can demonstrate that their achievements are acknowledged and valued. In order to do so, though, praise must be seen to be genuine and to be given for genuine effort. In other circumstances it is unhelpful, for it not only conveys low expectations, but also fails to clarify for the pupil the learning demands of the particular task.

Their curriculum-based assessments should alert teachers to the sorts of assistance that pupils will require in order to complete tasks successfully. For those with the most extensive difficulties it may be necessary to plan a structured programme of support, whereby they are helped to progress step by step towards increasingly independent learning as they gain in competence and confidence. For all children, though, there is a fine line to tread in judging what degree of teacher assistance and feedback is appropriate (Westwood 1997). Too little, and a pupil may become frustrated and lose confidence; too much, and the teacher may inadvertently foster undue dependency. It is to the benefit of neither teacher nor pupil if the latter learns to seek continuous reassurance that he or she is 'doing the right thing'. What is needed, rather, is an approach which encourages children to gain increasing self-management of their own learning (see, for example, Hart 1996; Jones and Charlton 1996). Such an approach, which is in line with the expectations of the Code of Practice for pupil involvement in the learning process, implies the need for teachers to give explicit focus in their planning to the development of strategies whereby pupils can monitor, review and begin to evaluate their own progress.

On the whole, the adaptations to teaching methods that have been outlined can be characterized as 'common sense' (Westwood 1997). That is, they primarily involve closer attention to aspects of planning which need to be considered for all pupils. However, if they are to be effective, then they must be used in a consistent and purposeful way, and the Code of Practice provides the framework for both planning and monitoring their implementation. Where reviews of pupil progress suggest that more intensive intervention is required, IEPs sometimes incorporate the use of more specialized methods. These can take the form of individualized or small group programmes, devised by the school's special educational needs coordinator (SENCO) and/or advisory teachers or educational psychologist. Where a pupil's difficulties lie in the acquisition of basic literacy and numeracy skills, for example, programmes are frequently based on a behavioural objectives approach. These will employ more carefully graded materials, more directive and structured teaching techniques, and a finer-grained recording of pupil progress than would ordinarily be needed. Such programmes may be implemented by the class teacher or by support staff, either within or outside the usual classroom context. The impact of these and other organizational strategies are discussed in the following section.

Organizational strategies

The degree of success that pupils experience in their learning is influenced not only by the nature of planned curricular tasks and teaching methods but also by contextual factors within the classroom. These include, for example, its physical organization, the timing and pacing of learning activities, the management of resources to support learning and the grouping of pupils.

A primary concern in considering the physical organization of the classroom must be the range and variety of curricular activities that are to take place there, and how the layout of the room can best facilitate both pupil engagement with these activities and teacher supervision and guidance of their learning. While attention to lighting, noise level, ease of access to equipment and resources, and mobility between different areas will be necessary in any classroom, it is particularly important where there are pupils with sensory or physical impairments. Furthermore, individual pupils are likely to have different levels of tolerance for what they find distracting in their environment: observational assessment should indicate whether there is a need, for example, for quieter or more sheltered working areas which can be used as required. Caution is needed, though, to ensure that these do not result in permanent physical segregation within the classroom of those pupils who find it difficult to concentrate.

Variations in pupils' pace of work, and in the extent of their need for assistance and for repeated practice or consolidation activities, raise significant issues for teachers concerning the management of time and resources. Here, it is not simply a question of the time or resources that are available, but the use to which they are put. It is not unusual to find, as Croll and Moses (1985) did in their study of junior classrooms, that on average children with special educational needs spend less time directly engaged with curricular activities, and correspondingly more time distracted from their work, than do their peers. As these are the very pupils who may be thought to require more time spent on task, this indicates a need for organizational and management strategies which enable maximum opportunities for teacher interaction with pupils and concentrated engagement with learning activities (Ainscow 1989).

This does not imply though that pupils with special educational needs necessarily require one-to-one attention from their teacher. Too often individual work has been seen as the only preferred means for responding to their learning difficulties, yet it is an approach which has its limitations. When well planned and managed, it allows a careful match to individual needs and can certainly enhance children's levels of task engagement. However, it is neither possible nor desirable for children to work in this way for much of their time. Even where they need to follow special individual learning programmes, these can only form a small part of their curriculum, for no matter how good the programmes are, if pupils spend most of their time in this way they are effectively being segregated from the rest of the class (Lewis 1995b). Where there is an absence of common ground and shared curricular experiences with peers, this denies children the learning support that they can gain from each other, and it can also exacerbate the social difficulties that those with special educational needs so often experience. It is important, therefore, to look at the balance of individual, group and class activities provided for all pupils and, in doing so, to recognize that peers can be a particularly significant learning resource in the classroom.

It is generally acknowledged that peers act as influential models for each other, and that peer acceptance and approval can be powerful incentives. Their potential teaching role is often used incidentally and informally in classrooms; for example, when one pupil is asked to explain or demonstrate an activity to another. It may, however, be formalized through peer-tutoring schemes (Topping 1988), where pupils are coached in a specific tutoring role, such as in reading, and paired with pupils to whom they then give regular individual help. Sometimes pupils are tutors to others in their own class, and sometimes to those who are younger. An interesting development has been in the involvement of older pupils who themselves have reading difficulties as tutors of younger children. Where these schemes have worked well, considerable benefits have been claimed both for those being tutored and also for the tutors, and the pupils have apparently enjoyed the experience. However, if peer-tutoring is to be successful, there is clearly a need for sensitivity, not only in the way in which the scheme is introduced but also in assessing which pupils will work constructively together. If pupils are to be tutored by others in their class, it is important that at other times they are seen to have their own contribution to make to paired or group learning.

In formal peer-tutoring arrangements, it is often reported that the paired pupils develop a mutual sense of purpose and a shared pleasure in achievement, and, furthermore, that the learning of both is enhanced. However, their relationship is essentially unequal, in so far as one is giving and the other receiving help. By contrast, a unique quality of peer relationships in general is that they involve more equal status than is true of adult–child or teacher–pupil interaction. As a result, peers can provide not only an alternative form of assistance, but can also make different learning demands of one another than those made by teachers. It is, for example, important for the development of their problem-solving strategies that pupils are exposed to alternative viewpoints, articulate, clarify and justify their own, and learn ways of reconciling differences in perspectives. There is some evidence that paired or small group activity can play a particularly important role here. For example, children have been reported to solve certain problems at a more advanced level when working cooperatively in pairs, whether of similar or dissimilar achievement, than when working independently (e.g. Foot *et al.* 1990). For this reason, there has been increasing interest in cooperative group work as a context for addressing a range of pupils' learning needs.

If it is to be successful, cooperative work requires careful planning because it entails an additional set of learning demands for the pupils to those that are implicit in the task itself. Putting children together and asking them to cooperate is clearly insufficient by itself, and teachers need to help them practise the necessary social and cooperative skills. Tasks need to be structured to promote 'positive interdependence' and individual accountability for the group's work (Putnam 1993), for example by 'jigsawing' them (Rose 1991) into different sub-tasks or through role allocation for different task elements. When well managed, cooperative group work has been reported to lead not only to improved academic attainment, but also to enhanced self-esteem and social relationships. It has, therefore, been recognized as a potentially powerful strategy for promoting the inclusion of children with special educational needs in mainstream classrooms (Slavin 1990).

The recognition of the role peers can play in helping one

another's learning has implications for the way in which pupils are organized into groups within the classroom and, indeed, within the school. Much debate has focused on the relative advantages and disadvantages of different forms of grouping, but the evidence from studies of cooperative learning suggests that, at least for some activities, 'mixed ability' groupings can be of benefit on academic, personal and social grounds. Those who advocate a greater use of mixed ability teaching argue that grouping by ability can adversely affect not only teacher expectations, but also pupils' perceptions of themselves as learners. Furthermore, it can convey a message that attainment, above all, is what is highly valued in the classroom, and may reinforce feelings of failure among those who find learning difficult. These are serious concerns for anyone committed to meeting the full range of pupils' needs, and it is vital that they are not overlooked at a time when the pressure to raise pupil achievement is leading to more widespread use of 'ability setting'. However, there is no doubt that even without the current trend, teachers have frequently found that for certain purposes it is a more effective strategy to group by level of attainment. What is most important in this sort of group work is that the criteria upon which groups are based fit the specific teaching purpose, and that groupings are reviewed and revised in the light of continuous assessment. Whatever organizational arrangements are made, it has been argued that a fundamental principle must be to provide within the classroom 'an atmosphere of encouragement, acceptance, respect for individual achievements and sensitivity to individual needs, in which all pupils can thrive' (NCC 1989b: 7). The extent to which a teacher is successful in doing this may well prove to be more important than the exact balance of different grouping arrangements which he or she employs, but a guiding principle must surely be that flexible groupings should be adopted to suit different teaching purposes.

A balance of individual, group and whole class work is increasingly seen as an effective way to make the most of teaching and learning opportunities in the classroom. Whole class activities can be a powerful means for building shared learning experiences but it is evident that teachers require both skill and sensitivity if they are to help all children to participate successfully. Furthermore, some pupils are likely to need additional support to do so. The organization of additional adult assistance plays a significant role in meeting the full range of pupils' needs. Individual pupils with statements of special educational need often have further help available in the classroom on an hourly or daily basis from designated learning support assistants. The way in which a class teacher manages this support must vary according to the pupil's particular needs. However, it is unlikely to help the pupil's inclusion and independence in the classroom if the learning support assistant is always engaged in a one-to-one supervisory role. Increasingly, therefore, it has been accepted that supplementary assistance of this kind should be managed flexibly if it is to enhance the learning opportunities that are provided (Balshaw 1991; Lorenz 1996). There is, though, rather more argument regarding the most appropriate organization of specialist or additional teacher help for those experiencing learning difficulties. Here, the central issue has been whether it should be given by 'in-class support' or by sessional withdrawal of pupils from the classroom, and accordingly this involves school policy rather more than the individual decisions of particular teachers.

The use of in-class support has been associated with a whole school approach to provision for pupils with special educational needs because it can be argued that it should ensure that all class teachers maintain responsibility for their learning. By contrast, when a withdrawal system is operated, this responsibility may be seen as resting solely with the staff who support the pupils outside the classroom. It has frequently been suggested that withdrawal can lead to pupils being negatively labelled, although it should be pointed out that this may also result from visible and identifiably 'special' support within the classroom. Perhaps most significantly, however, poorly timed and badly coordinated withdrawal can result in considerable disruption to a pupil's learning in other curricular activities. Thus, for example, pupils may be withdrawn from lessons in which they could develop real strengths, or may miss the practical sessions which they return to find the rest of their class discussing. Where there is little or no coordination between support teacher and class teachers, and scant attention to the way in which classwork and support work should be integrated, then clearly withdrawal must be viewed as unsatisfactory. However, a more positive system of withdrawal is possible, and when flexibly used need not be incompatible with a whole school approach.

For withdrawal to be used constructively, it should be characterized by regular joint planning and review between all the teachers concerned, so that the support pupils receive is followed through into the classroom. Furthermore, the withdrawal sessions must be sensitively timed in order to minimize disruption and to ensure that pupils still benefit from the full range of curricular experience. Some children are likely to find it easier to concentrate on particular sorts of support activity in a quiet withdrawal room, and feel more comfortable asking for help and guidance in a smaller group context. In such circumstances, or where the support activities themselves might be disruptive to the rest of the class, then withdrawal can be an effective strategy. In other situations, however, in-class support allows greater potential flexibility in the way class teacher and support teacher work together, and the assistance given to the pupil can be integrated more readily with the curricular activities of the rest of the class. Nevertheless, it must be acknowledged that effective in-class support is not without its difficulties. Thomas (1992), for example, has drawn attention to the obstacles which can prevent successful teamwork within the classroom, and it is evident that it requires considerable commitment to cooperative planning and teaching from all the staff concerned. In their study of secondary schools, Lee and Henkhuzens (1996) reported that among schools identified by their LEAs as examples of 'good practice', in-class support predominated, but almost all also used withdrawal for certain purposes. A prime concern wherever the support takes place is the quality of help to the learner: as pupils become more involved in the development and review of their IEPs, then it is important to ensure that their own perspectives on this are taken into account.

Classroom relationships

An emphasis on the importance of positive and cooperative classroom relationships, between teachers and pupils and between the pupils themselves, has been implicit in much of the preceding discussion. There is a complex interaction between personal, social and more academic aspects of learning and it is not surprising to find that pupils who experience problems with the demands made by the formal curriculum in school may often also demonstrate difficulties in their personal and social relationships. Pupils with special educational needs have an even stronger need than others for positive and supportive attitudes from staff, and for the provision of a classroom climate in which 'all pupils feel valued and able to risk making mistakes as they learn, without fear of criticism' (NCC 1989b: 8).

In schools and classrooms where expectations of children with special educational needs are low, and they both perceive themselves and are seen by their peers as failures, this is likely to have a negative effect not only on their self-esteem and confidence, but also on their enthusiasm and motivation for learning and for cooperation with others. By contrast, positive expectations and confidence in themselves as learners may do much to promote their achievements, and in learning environments where their efforts and achievements are recognized and genuinely valued, their personal and social development can be enhanced. A more detailed consideration of the social and emotional climate of classroom relationships forms the focus of the next chapter.

Discussion points

1   Select a task which you would plan for a group of pupils. Then (i) attempt to analyse the skills, knowledge and concepts that the task requires; and (ii) outline a sequence of activities through which these might be taught. Consider the strengths and limitations of this form of task analysis as an aid to planning.

2   Use your analysis as a framework for considering what sorts of assessment evidence you would need in order to establish appropriate starting points for teaching the selected task, and to identify potential areas of difficulty that pupils might experience.

3   Lewis (1995b) has argued that there is little merit in pretending that differences in attainment do not exist, for the pupils will certainly be aware of them. With respect to their classroom relationships and their approach to learning, consider what might be the impact on pupils with special educational needs of 'ability' and 'mixed ability' groupings.

Further reading

Lewis, A. (1995) *Primary Special Needs and the National Curriculum*, 2nd edn, London: Routledge.

Sewell, G. (1996) *Special Needs Provision: Assessment, Concern and Action*, London: Cassell.

Westwood, P. (1997) *Commonsense Methods for Children with Special Needs*, 3rd edn, London: Routledge.

Chapter 6

The social and emotional context for learning

An interactive concept of special educational needs emphasizes that pupils experience difficulties where there is a significant mismatch between what they themselves bring to bear in learning situations and the expectations that are made of them. In the previous chapters, attention has primarily been focused on the learning demands of the formal curriculum. It should be acknowledged, however, that the informal or 'hidden' curriculum of relationships and interactions at school can also pose considerable demands of pupils with respect to their social competence and their personal resources, such as self-confidence. The interrelationships between children's learning achievements and their social and personal development are complex, but it is generally accepted that pupils learn most effectively when they feel valued and secure, trust their teachers, and both understand and accept the full range of classroom demands (Pollard 1988). For all pupils, therefore, there is a need to consider the social context and emotional climate for learning that classrooms and schools provide. However, this may be particularly important for those with special educational needs.

Children with learning difficulties

Where children repeatedly experience failure in their learning, this will almost certainly have a negative impact on their self-esteem. They are likely to begin to doubt their own competence as learners, and see any successes they have as arising from factors outside their control. In such situations, they may feel anxious, frustrated and personally helpless, or they may start to view curricular tasks as boring and irrelevant and become disaffected with classroom learning (Galloway 1990). It should not be surprising then if, in order to retain a personal sense of worth, they develop strategies of task avoidance, for example by passive withdrawal from their engagement with learning activities or by more overt distraction and disruption of the work of their peers. However, it must be stressed that it is by no means inevitable that children with learning difficulties demonstrate such problems. When positive steps are taken to provide appropriate guidance and support, they can be helped to experience regular success, to monitor and gain confidence in their own developing competence, and to see that their achievements are valued. Nevertheless, pupils with learning difficulties are frequently also described by their teachers as showing emotional and behavioural difficulties, and where this is so, it is important to be alert to the potential contribution that can be made by the climate of attitudes, expectations and relationships within the classroom.

Teacher attitudes towards and expectations of pupils, and the extent to which these are communicated, are fundamentally important. They can influence not only the way in which individual pupils perceive themselves, but also the way that they are viewed by their peers. The attitudes and behaviour that teachers demonstrate towards pupils with learning difficulties are, as discussed previously, affected by a range of factors. These include their knowledge, information and understanding of special educational needs, their confidence in their own professional competence to meet the full range of those needs, and the quality and availability of any necessary additional support. However, it seems central to the development of a positive attitude that, first, needs are recognized as predominantly interactive in nature, rather than as fixed and unchangeable characteristics of a child, and, second, that while individual differences are acknowledged and respected, these are neither unnecessarily emphasized nor allowed to result in an inappropriate lowering of expectations.

If teachers are to plan and organize their teaching in a way which is responsive to individual need, they do of course need to develop differential expectations of different pupils. What seems most important, though, is that these expectations are founded on accurate information and are realistically high. Furthermore, teachers should be aware of the expectations that they hold, and must be prepared to adapt these flexibly on the basis of their continuous assessment. Of course, it is not only the expectations that teachers hold but also the ways in which these are communicated to pupils that are significant. They can be demonstrated both verbally and non-verbally, for example, by the learning tasks teachers set, the feedback they give and the nature of the individual attention they provide.

It has often been argued that children tend to conform to the expectations that are conveyed by their teachers. Low expectations which are likely to have a cumulative adverse effect can be communicated when teachers resort to frequent negative criticism of work. This is particularly damaging if the criticism focuses on the pupil as a learner, rather than on task-related guidance as to how he or she might become more successful. By contrast, when teachers give supportive and constructive critical feedback, in which they draw attention to personal effort and progress and acknowledge individual achievement, their strategies may do much to promote pupils' learning. Teacher behaviour which appears positive does not always demonstrate high expectations, however. Smith and Laslett (1993) have pointed out that some well-intentioned teacher responses to individual need can inadvertently act to reinforce a pupil's feelings of inadequacy or difference from his or her peers. They caution that oversimplified questioning, the provision of activities which are obviously different from those for the rest of the class, and the use of indiscriminate praise for inadequate work are often symptomatic of inappropriately low expectations. On the whole, then, it appears that if teachers are to communicate positive expectations of pupils, this can be best achieved where any necessary adaptations to their teaching approach are made in as unobtrusive a manner as possible, and where attention is focused on individual progress rather than on comparisons with peers.

A positive learning environment, in which all pupils feel that they are valued members of a mutually supportive class group, is fundamentally associated with the quality of relationships within the classroom. This embraces not only teacher–pupil relationships, but also those between the pupils themselves. Good peer relationships are important for children's personal and social development, and, as discussed in the previous chapter, pupils can act as influential models and tutors for one another's learning. However, it is often pointed out that, in schools and classes where academic attainment and competitiveness are the only predominant values, children with learning difficulties are likely to have poor status among their peers. If teachers wish to foster a classroom climate in which expectations are realistically high, and in which all pupils are respected as individuals and all feel they have a worthwhile contribution to make, it is essential that cooperative aspects of learning and non-academic achievements are also given an appropriate emphasis.

Emotional and behavioural difficulties at school

Within any school there will be some pupils who have greater difficulties than others in meeting the personal and social demands that are made of them. These pupils may need additional help in order to establish positive relationships with their teachers and their peers. They are likely to include, for example, children who feel vulnerable or insecure, those with poorly developed social skills and others who have learned inappropriate strategies for gaining attention (Fontana 1985). Whether they demonstrate their difficulties through passive or more overt forms of behaviour, they can often have a considerable impact on the general climate of classroom relationships. Where their problems in adjusting to the social and personal demands of school persist, and are such as to interfere with their own learning, the learning of their peers or their teacher's organizational and management strategies, they are likely to be identified as having emotional or behavioural difficulties.

It is clear that a wide range of interacting factors can contribute to emotional and behavioural difficulties. These include the child's health and temperament, home and family circumstances and wider community influences. While not denying the significance of these factors, it should, however, be acknowledged that schools and classrooms can also play an important part. It is necessary, therefore, that teachers are alert to those aspects of school life that may influence the difficulties that pupils experience, and, furthermore, that they seek to identify those that might be amenable to change (Galloway 1990; Cooper *et al.* 1994).

We may all behave differently in different contexts. Furthermore, any individual might show problematic behaviour in certain situations. It follows, then, that 'difficult' behaviour at school cannot be viewed in isolation from the context in which it occurs. Schools and teachers can vary in the value judgements they bring to bear when defining particular behaviour as problematic, and also in the way they respond to these. There is evidence too that schools vary in their effectiveness in establishing and maintaining appropriate standards of behaviour (Rutter *et al.* 1979). It has therefore been increasingly recognized that both the formal curriculum and the general ethos of a school can have a considerable impact on pupil behaviour. As a result, attention has been drawn to the need for 'whole school' policies which aim to minimize the likelihood that pupils will experience emotional or behavioural difficulties, and to develop strategies which will alleviate rather than aggravate those problems which do arise (Galvin *et al.* 1990). There have been growing concerns about the number and range of behavioural difficulties in mainstream schools and the concomitant rise in permanent exclusions (Garner 1993). LEAs are therefore required to develop Behaviour Support Plans which include details of the support they provide for schools in relation to the management of pupil behaviour. Schools themselves must have written discipline policies. Against this background context, it has been suggested that teachers may generally be more alert to overt forms of disruption than to signs of emotional withdrawal at school. However, a broad-based school policy which is designed to promote positive behaviour should provide a secure learning context which will help all pupils develop their personal resources and social relationships.

The exact form that such a policy takes will obviously vary according to the strengths of the school staff and the needs of the pupils. However, the Elton Report on discipline in schools (DES 1989) sets out some important principles. It recommends that the pupils themselves should be involved in the process of development and review of school policy, and that there should also be close liaison with their parents as well as with other agencies. The main aim of the policy should be to create a 'positive atmosphere based on a sense of community and a shared sense of values' (ibid.: 13), where rules are clearly communicated and agreed. Explicit consideration should be given in the school curriculum to the development of mutual respect, responsibility and self-discipline. The

Report points out that this necessitates that personal and social as well as academic aspects of learning are monitored, and that the full range of pupils' achievements is given due recognition. However, it emphasizes that no matter how carefully designed the school policy is, its successful implementation will depend on the quality of teacher–pupil relationships and on the establishment of effective classroom management.

Teacher–pupil relationships and classroom management

Positive teacher–pupil relationships are fundamental to effective classroom management, because any strategies a teacher employs will be more successful in a climate of mutual trust and respect. The extent to which teachers demonstrate genuine interest in pupils as individuals, as well as care and concern for the class as a whole, is reflected in their planning, organization and management of learning experiences. It is clear that problematic behaviour is less likely to arise in lessons which maximize pupils' engagement with curricular activities, because this automatically reduces the opportunity for disruption. Planning for this level of task involvement implies an explicit consideration of both individual and full class needs. For example, where pupils have difficulties in peer relationships which interfere with their learning, it is important not only to help them as individuals to develop their confidence and social skills, but also to work with the class as a whole in order to ensure that they do not become the subject of teasing, ridicule or rejection. Similarly, when pupils have learning difficulties, there is a need to promote their self-esteem and their motivation for learning by the provision of relevant and achievable tasks, and by regular constructive feedback and praise. It should be apparent, though, that the value of such strategies is not confined to those with difficulties, for all pupils are likely to show more enthusiasm for and involvement in curricular activities when the full range of personal and cooperative achievements is seen to be positively valued.

In order to establish effective classroom management, however, it is important that teachers should not only provide positive feedback to pupils on their curricular achievements, but also on their behaviour. It is often reported that teachers are generally sparing with their praise for personal and social conduct, and give far more attention to misbehaviour. A positive approach to classroom management (e.g. Galvin *et al.* 1990) is very different from this, because it is based on the premise that it is more effective to reward the keeping of rules than it is to punish their infringement. From this perspective, pupils need to be clear about what their teachers expect and why, and should receive positive rather than negative feedback to clarify how far they are meeting these expectations. A starting point, therefore, is the establishment of explicit and agreed rules and routines which can be regularly reviewed with the class. These should be framed in positive terms, such as 'we sit quietly in assembly', 'we walk along the corridor', 'we listen when others are talking'. Then, instead of drawing attention to the rules when they are broken, a strategy is used which is often referred to as 'catch them being good'. That is, the rules are reinforced by actively looking for appropriate behaviour and rewarding it, with the aim of keeping the climate as positive as possible in the classroom.

Even in such a positive climate, problems can obviously arise. Through their general sensitivity to the mood of the class, as well as through their active scanning and monitoring, teachers can be alerted to situations where this might happen. They can also seek to anticipate and avoid unnecessary conflicts. Smith and Laslett (1993) have suggested that the pupils themselves often may not be aware of why they are misbehaving, but they note that minor misdemeanours may escalate into more disruptive incidents unless teachers take prompt action to prevent this. The strategies teachers employ should avoid the sort of threats or disparaging remarks that are likely to back both teachers and pupils into a corner. That is, they must provide a way of 'saving face' for all concerned, if problems are not to escalate. The aim, then, will be to demonstrate that the teacher is in control of, rather than merely reacting to, the situation. It is evident that different strategies will be more successful with some pupils than others, but Smith and Laslett suggest that a general principle must be to 'nip trouble in the bud'; that is, to move quickly to inhibit any inappropriate behaviour before it becomes more widespread. This is likely to be most effective when it is done in as quiet, good-humoured and matter-of-fact a way as possible. Thus the pupil should be reminded in positive terms of the rules and routines, and be redirected without more ado to the task in hand.

Figure 6.1 provides extracts from a positive behaviour policy which was developed by the staff of an infant school. As its guidelines on 'rules, praise and ignoring' make clear, there will be times in any classroom when further sanctions or punishments are required. However, following a positive approach to class management, in order to minimize these, the balance of attention should be given to the reinforcement of appropriate conduct. It is worthwhile considering, therefore, why rewards should be thought to be more effective than punishments. First, what teachers and pupils view as punishments may not correspond. Topping (1983), for example, has reported that frequent verbal reprimand may actually serve to reinforce disruptive behaviour. It might be noted, though, that a similar discrepancy can also occur between teachers and pupils on what constitutes reward: for instance, some pupils may be embarrassed by being singled out for praise in front of their peers. Where such a mismatch exists between teacher intentions and pupil perceptions, the teacher's use of both praise and reprimand may be equally ineffective. A further argument that can be made against the use of punishment is that it acts to focus undue attention on inappropriate behaviour, rather than providing pupils with models of appropriate conduct. Perhaps the strongest concerns, though, relate to the adverse effect that it can have on teacher–pupil relationships. If this is to be minimized, any punishments must be carried out both sensitively and fairly, and also within the framework of a more positive approach. Docking (1989) has emphasized that the focus should be on the reasonableness of the rule that has been infringed, and the teacher's manner should convey that it is the behaviour rather than the pupil that is unacceptable. Further, the reasons for any sanction should be made explicit, and the pupil concerned should be provided with guidance and help to meet the expected standards of behaviour.

Specific strategies for managing problematic behaviour

The emphasis of a positive approach to classroom management is on the prevention of difficult or disruptive behaviour. However, in some cases the extent of a pupil's problematic behaviour will be such as to require more individualized attention. Where this is so it

We wish to provide an ethos of mutual respect, self-respect, independence, responsibility and self-motivation.

We believe that good behaviour goes hand in hand with good relationships and that positive rules, negotiated with all concerned and backed by praise and rewards, will help achieve this aim.

Rules, praise and ignoring – guidelines

1 Agree with the class four or five rules and display these on the walls where they can easily be seen.
2 ... [the rules] should tell the children what they should do rather than what they should not do.
3 Instead of telling them off when they break the rules ... praise them for keeping to the rules – this may seem somewhat unnatural at first.
4 When you praise them, tell them what it is that they are doing right
5 Use praise more than you normally would to begin with and try to make your praise statements outweigh your telling-offs by at least 3 to 1. Make your praise varied and sincere.
6 Try to ignore children who are breaking the rules but praise a child nearby who is keeping to the rules so that the rule breaker can hear you do this. Praise the errant pupil when he/she begins behaving appropriately.
7 If behaviour can't be ignored, remind the child of the rule and give a warning that if it is broken then ... (one of the school's agreed sanctions will be applied).
8 Praise this child when he/she begins following the rule again and keep him/her on task by using more praise.
9 If the child ignores the warning ... (then the agreed sanction is applied).

Figure 6.1 Extracts from an infant school's positive behaviour policy

is necessary to gather observational evidence of the nature of the pupil's difficulties in order to determine what sort of intervention might be appropriate. It is important to acknowledge that objective appraisal of behaviour which may be both challenging and under-mining of one's confidence can be difficult. It can often be the case that teachers become selectively sensitive to the behaviour of a pupil who gives them cause for concern, and accordingly they may only be alert to his or her inappropriate behaviour rather than to those positive aspects that could be built upon. Furthermore, behaviour which might be ignored in another pupil may be perceived as problematic in that child, and if this leads to overt differences in teachers' reactions it can serve to reinforce a class perception that the individual, rather than his or her behaviour, is a problem. For these reasons it is helpful to structure one's observa-tions in such a way as to focus systematically on specific aspects of the behaviour that gives concern. One possible framework which has been suggested (Leach and Raybould 1977) centres on the following questions: how far does the behaviour interfere with the pupil's learning and that of others? How different is it from the behaviour of others in the class? How often does it occur and how long does it last? From the pupil's point of view, how reasonable is it in the situations in which it occurs? In how many and what sort of situations does it occur? The answers to questions of this kind should help inform a teacher's assessment of the seriousness of the pupil's difficulties and the need for systematic intervention. They can also provide a basis for discussion and consultation with colleagues, the pupil and the pupil's parents about the appropriate steps that should be taken. Where systematic intervention is decided upon, this should be planned, monitored and reviewed using the framework of an Individual Educational Plan (IEP).

Behavioural strategies

Behavioural strategies have an influential role in many intervention approaches for children showing problematic behaviour. The princi-ples which underpin them are that behaviour which is reinforced tends to be repeated and, conversely, that behaviour which is not reinforced will become less frequent. It should be apparent that these principles are closely associated with a positive approach to general classroom management. It is widely accepted, though, that behavioural approaches can have an important role to play not only in the establishment of appropriate conduct but also in the reduction of inappropriate behaviour.

Where pupils show persistent difficulties that cannot be overcome by general management procedures, a structured behavioural approach begins with a detailed observational analysis of incidents of appropriate and inappropriate behaviour. In recording these, particular attention is given to:

(i)   the specific situation(s) in which the behaviour occurs;
(ii) the behaviour itself, described in objective and precise terms; and
(iii) the consequences of the behaviour, including both teacher and peer responses.

An analysis of the situations in which different sorts of behaviour are observed may reveal that a pupil's inappropriate behaviour is more likely to occur in some contexts than in others. It might be, for example, that it is more strongly associated with certain pupil groupings than others, or with particular demands, such as the sharing of materials. In some cases, this will indicate that minor environmental modifications can be made in order to promote appropriate and inhibit inappropriate behaviour. More generally, though, it will serve to direct a teacher's attention to those contexts which a pupil seems to find particularly problematic.

The analysis of the consequences of a pupil's behaviour is based on certain assumptions: first, that problem behaviour is being reinforced in the classroom in some way; and, conversely, that more appropriate behaviour may be receiving little or no reinforcement. It might be the case, for example, that inappropriate behaviour results in a pupil receiving individual attention, whereas the expected and accepted forms of behaviour are ignored. Where this is so, it could be argued that what are intended by the teacher as reprimands or sanctions actually serve to reinforce misconduct. Such a hypothesis leads to a plan of action in which the pattern of reinforcement is changed, so that attention is given to appropriate behaviour and withdrawn from unacceptable behaviour. This form of strategy is central to a behavioural approach, for it views acceptable and unacceptable behaviour as essentially incompatible: the increase of one is explicitly linked with the decrease of the other. Any behavioural intervention must therefore aim to increase the incidence of appropriate behaviour and at the same time to reduce the occurrence of problematic behaviour.

In order to increase appropriate behaviour, from this perspective, it may be sufficient to apply the 'catch them being good' strategy, provided that this is done in a consistent and structured way. In some cases, though, there may be few if any occasions when a child can be 'caught being good'. This situation usually arises where the gap between a pupil's existing behaviour and that which is expected in the classroom is too great to be achievable in one step. Where this is so, it is necessary to outline the stages through which it might be attained. For example, if a pupil is really 'always' out of his or her seat, then it is unrealistic to view 'remaining in seat throughout the lesson' as an immediately achievable goal. However, if intermediate goals are planned and discussed with the pupil, he or she will know what to aim for, and can be rewarded for steps along the way which come successively closer to this. In order to be effective, it is important that the pupil not only understands the requirements that are being made, but is also helped to monitor his or her own progress towards the longer-term goal. Furthermore, if teacher attention and praise are not found sufficiently rewarding, other forms of reinforcement, such as the privilege of additional time on a preferred activity, will be needed.

Behavioural strategies for decreasing inappropriate behaviour in the classroom depend upon the analysis of what seems to have been maintaining this. If individual attention, even of a negative kind, has been identified as a contributing factor, then 'planned ignoring' may be used. There are a number of situations in which this is clearly not an appropriate strategy, however, such as in those instances where the ignored behaviour is likely to spread to the pupil's peers, or where the behaviour itself puts the pupil or others at risk. In other circumstances, if planned ignoring is to be effective, it must be consistently applied and should be coupled with the giving of attention for positive behaviour. It should be noted, though, that although it can be an effective strategy, it does often lead to an initial escalation of inappropriate behaviour. Moreover, it will usually require careful explanation, not only to the pupil concerned, but also to others in the class upon whose cooperation its success may depend.

Attention can also be withdrawn from a pupil by the use of 'time out', in which the pupil is removed from the context of general classroom activities to a safe and supervised, but unstimulating, area. In order to be successfully applied, this strategy needs to be fully understood by the pupil, and it should be carried out in a matter-of-fact way and for a brief pre-specified period only, after which the pupil should be welcomed back into classroom activities, with no further discussion of the misbehaviour. It is important to note that this strategy differs in a number of significant ways from the far less carefully considered approach of sending children out of the room until the end of a lesson, and reprimanding them subsequently.

The use of 'planned ignoring' will only be effective if teacher and peer attention is perceived as a reinforcement to a pupil. Similarly, 'time out' is likely to be successful only when 'time in' the classroom is rewarding. Where observational analysis has not clearly indicated the influence of teacher or peer attention on a pupil's behaviour, then from a behavioural perspective it follows that it will be necessary to identify other incentives or privileges which not only can be awarded for appropriate behaviour but can also be withdrawn for inappropriate behaviour. Often this involves some form of contract between teacher and pupil, and in some situations parental cooperation may also be sought to help implement the strategy.

Whichever strategies are adopted, the behavioural model emphasizes a carefully planned step-by-step approach, in which achievable targets are set at each stage and the pupil is helped to recognize his or her own progress. More detailed discussion of the application of behavioural techniques can be found in a number of sources (e.g. Wheldall and Merrett 1984; Montgomery 1989; Rogers 1994).

Wider approaches

The strengths of the behavioural approach lie in its focus on positive changes which can be achieved within the classroom. It provides a clear structure for observational assessment of the nature of the behaviour causing concern and of the classroom-based factors that may contribute to its occurrence. It has been discussed at some length because it provides a valuable resource for teachers. However, it should not be used in isolation because by itself it has some significant limitations. These arise from its basis in an over-simplified model of human behaviour. As a result, it does not take account of the many complex interacting influences on pupils not only within the classroom and throughout the school but also in wider family and community contexts.

An acknowledgement of the impact on pupils' behaviour of rela-tionships within school and between school and other contexts implies the need for the sort of broader, multifaceted approach referred to by Cooper *et al.* (1994) as ecosystemic. Such an approach has clear parallels with the ecological perspective on curriculum development discussed in Chapter 4. It incorporates attention to individual behaviour, but also involves detailed consideration of the constructive changes that could be made in the classroom and school environment to promote positive interactions. It is an approach which is consistent with the principles of the Code of Practice (DfE 1994a) because, in addition, it emphasizes the impor-tance of close liaison between school staff, with parents and, where appropriate, with other agencies.

As the Code makes clear, there should also be full involvement of the pupils themselves in setting aims, planning and evaluating strategies to enhance their behaviour, and recording their own progress. This means that any intervention must take account of two further aspects which are not addressed by the behavioural approach. First, it should be recognized that there can be a strong emotional component to the sorts of behaviour which cause teachers concern. For example, children who are identified as having emotional and behavioural difficulties are often ill at ease with their own response to the personal and social demands of school, but anxiety or lack of confidence can lead them to be reluc-tant to admit to their difficulties or seek help. In such cases, they are likely to need the opportunity to both express their feelings and listen to those of others through supportive contexts, such as 'circle time' (Mosley 1993). Second, children should be encouraged to become self-aware and to monitor and manage their own behaviour, rather than simply to respond to external control. They need to learn to anticipate and understand the consequences of their own actions, and to acquire sensitivity to the needs and rights of others. This may involve the use of cognitive strategies, which help children to clarify and assess their own perceptions of problematic situations, and to appraise their strengths and needs in responding to these (e.g. Galvin 1989; Rogers 1994). It might be noted though that, while such an approach can be related to the requirements of the Code of Practice, it is far from unique to those experiencing special educational needs. The provision of learning experiences in which pupils are helped to gain increased understanding not only of their own achievements, rights and responsibilities but also those of others is fundamental to personal and social education (Galloway 1990).

Discussion points

1   Outline the rules that you would wish to establish with a class group. Consider how effectively the 'catch them being good' strategy might be applied to reinforce these.
2   A privilege can be given to reward appropriate behaviour, or alternatively it can be withdrawn as a sanction for inappropriate behaviour. Discuss what form privileges might take. In doing so, consider the distinction that should be made between pupils' privileges and pupils' rights. For example, should playtimes be regarded as a privilege which can be withdrawn?
3   Discuss which teaching strategies are likely to be most and least effective in promoting a pupil's sense of personal worth.

Further reading

Cooper, P., Smith, C. and Upton, G. (1994) *Emotional and Behavioural Difficulties: From Theory to Practice*, London: Routledge.
Smith, C. and Laslett, R. (1993) *Effective Classroom Management*, 2nd edn, London: Routledge.

Chapter 7

Frameworks of support

Throughout the preceding chapters it has been emphasized that special educational provision must be seen as integral to the work of a school. It follows then that all teachers are teachers of pupils with special educational needs, with a central role not only in their identification and assessment but also in developing classroom strategies to meet these needs. This has implications both for the initial training of teachers and also for their continuing professional development, and the national standards which have recently been introduced by the Teacher Training Agency (TTA) reflect this. For example, standards introduced for newly qualified teachers in 1998 emphasize that they should understand their responsibilities under the terms of the Code of Practice, be able to identify children's special educational needs and, with support, differentiate their teaching strategies as required. Furthermore, following a supported induction year, they should be able to plan appropriately to meet special educational needs and work effectively with support staff in the classroom and with the children's parents (DfEE 1998a). Standards have also been drawn up for experienced staff working as special educational needs coordinators (SENCOs) which outline a framework of competencies for their professional development (TTA 1998). Further standards are also planned for specialist SEN teachers. Over time, these initiatives are likely to have an impact on the confidence and competence of school staffs and the development of whole school approaches to meeting special educational needs. Nevertheless, in order to fulfil their roles most effectively, teachers will continue to need access to advice, support and expertise to supplement and complement their own knowledge and skills. The exact nature of the help available to teachers varies from area to area, but sources of support include colleagues on the school staff, professionals from outside agencies who work within the school, other professionals who liaise with the school and, finally and importantly, the pupils' parents.

Any network of support is only likely to be effective where there is clear understanding and communication about the complementary roles and responsibilities of all concerned in meeting pupils' needs. In the following discussion it should be borne in mind that support services, and the names given to these, vary from authority to authority, and furthermore that professionals with the same job title may not always approach their work in the same way. Nevertheless, some common features can be described in the pattern of support both within and outside school.

Colleagues on the school staff

All schools must have a special educational needs policy which should spell out the way in which their special educational provision is made. Where schools take seriously the importance of a whole school approach, it follows that many colleagues, including, for example, subject specialists and those with pastoral responsibilities, may provide help and advice in developing strategies to meet individual needs. The number of staff with particular expertise and specific responsibilities in this area will vary according to the size and nature of the school. However, all schools should have a designated member of staff, usually referred to as the SENCO, whose role it is to develop, coordinate and review the provision that is made. The Code of Practice (DfE 1994a) identifies seven key areas of responsibility as follows: the day-to-day operation of the school's SEN policy; liaising with and advising fellow teachers; coordinating provision for children with special educational needs; maintaining the school's SEN register and overseeing the records on all pupils with special educational needs; liaising with parents of children with special educational needs; contributing to the in-service training of staff; and liaising with external agencies.

It is a large and complex task and perhaps inevitably there can be tensions and dilemmas within a school about which elements should predominate (Dyson and Gains 1995). This is a particular issue in small schools where SENCOs typically have a range of other teaching responsibilities and little time allocated to the developmental aspects of their role. By comparison, in some larger schools, there may not just be one SENCO but a learning support team. Whatever the school context though, the role needs to be developed with attention to a balance between two key aims: that is, to arrange and monitor interventions for those pupils who experience learning difficulties, but at the same time to prevent such difficulties from arising unnecessarily by contributing to the development of procedures and strategies that are inclusive of all pupils. In relation to the first of these aims, the SENCO coordinates the identification and assessment of pupils with special educational needs, develops appropriate resource materials, helps colleagues plan Individual Educational Plans (IEPs) and review their effectiveness, oversees the monitoring of the pupils' progress, and liaises and consults with school staff, support agencies and the pupils' parents. The second aim incorporates a responsibility to raise colleagues' awareness of special educational needs and to work actively with them to ensure that the curriculum is accessible to all pupils and that any unnecessary barriers to learning are overcome.

Much of the role involves liaison with and support of colleagues, and the amount of time, if any, allocated to direct teaching of pupils varies in different schools. However, SENCOs and, in larger schools, other special needs teachers may withdraw individuals or small groups from lessons for specific purposes, as well as offering support within the class. Whatever form such additional assistance takes, it should not be viewed as a means by which class teachers relinquish their responsibility for the pupils' progress. Rather, it is generally agreed that direct support is most successful when the reciprocal roles of class teacher and special needs teacher are acknowledged and clearly defined. It is important, therefore, that the support that is given is based on joint planning, in which both teachers bring their own knowledge and skills to bear.

In most schools, learning support assistants are employed and make a significant contribution to special educational provision. They work often, but not exclusively, to support pupils with statements. Their numbers have increased over a number of years, and the full-time equivalent of over 24,000 assistants were recently reported to be working in mainstream schools (DfEE 1997a). There has been a great deal of concern about the patchy nature of training opportunities for these staff, and some much needed national guidance is planned on both their induction and training and also the effective development of their role (DfEE 1998a). Although the work that they do is obviously partly determined by the nature of particular pupils' difficulties, it is not unusual to find some lack of clarity about constructive patterns of support. Too often they have worked primarily in an intensive one-to-one way with pupils which effectively segregates them from the rest of the class. However, as discussed in Chapter 5, additional classroom assistance is most effective where it is employed flexibly to support the teacher in meeting pupils' needs.

LEA support services

Advisory and support service

In most LEAs, a special needs advisor coordinates the work of an advisory and support service which is staffed primarily by specialist teachers. They work with groups of schools and, typically, also contribute to staff development programmes. Specialist learning support teachers are experienced in working with children with learning difficulties. They can provide both direct teaching input and also advice and support; for example, on curriculum materials and resources, and the development of appropriate programmes of work. In some authorities there are also separate teams of specialist teachers for language support and, increasingly, for behavioural support who work in a similar way. Specialist teachers of hearing and visual impairment generally work directly with pupils, liaise with their parents and provide advice to school staff. They often work outside the classroom, where their input is mainly concerned with assessment and monitoring of hearing or vision, provision of aids and the supervision of their use. In addition, they may offer counselling to the pupils. They can provide information for school staff about the nature of a pupil's difficulties, and advice on the use and maintenance of aids. Importantly, they can also give guidance on strategies for the organization of the classroom, and on ways of ensuring access to the curriculum.

Schools Psychological Service

The Schools Psychological Service is staffed by educational psychologists, often working with social workers and specialist teachers. The educational psychologists are involved extensively in statutory assessment procedures: they must contribute to all formal assessments of special educational need and, where statements are maintained for pupils, to their annual reviews and reassessments. They frequently also have responsibility for collating the assessments made by other professionals and advising the LEA on the type of special educational provision that should be made. This limits the time they have for their other work with schools, and it is notable that, in order to strengthen the support available during the school-based stages of the Code of Practice, the government proposes to explore ways of redressing this balance (DfEE 1998a). Usually, educational psychologists are only asked for assistance with individual pupils when their needs cannot be met by the school's internal support systems. If appropriate, they work with the pupil's parents as well as with school staff and any other involved professionals, in order to determine strategies for meeting the pupil's needs. In addition to work on individual cases, however, educational psychologists can also undertake a wide range of other activities in school, including staff development work on issues such as behaviour management, the teaching of social skills, counselling and home–school liaison. In doing so, the aim is to help school staffs develop their own strengths in responding to the full range of their pupils' needs. Accordingly, in some authorities schools are allocated an amount of time from the psychological service, and can negotiate how that time might be used most effectively to meet whole school needs.

Special school staff

The recognition that special school staff might act as a potential source of support for mainstream colleagues dates back to the Warnock Report (DES 1978). It recommended closer working relationships between ordinary and special schools and, furthermore, that some special schools should be formally established as resource centres which could offer guidance and practical advice. This recommendation was not systematically adopted across the country, but a survey ten years later (Jowett *et al.* 1988) found that the vast majority of special schools had some sort of link with their neighbourhood schools. Where this has been most successful, the staffs of both schools derive valuable support and assistance from one another. Such links are likely to be developed further: within the context of its encouragement of greater inclusion, the government has emphasized that special schools should explore new roles and relationships with mainstream schools, for example through the sharing of teaching expertise, resources and facilities and through mutual support (DfEE 1997a).

The Educational Welfare Service

Traditionally, the work of educational welfare officers has been mainly concerned with school attendance, but in some authorities they have also played a significant part in supporting children with special educational needs and their families. Their contacts with families may alert them to potential difficulties. They can, therefore, bring to teachers' attention any adverse circumstances in pupils' lives outside school which may affect their learning and behaviour at school. They also represent a valuable link between education and health and social services.

Social services support

Social services departments not only have responsibilities for child care and protection, but are also involved more extensively with both families and wider neighbourhood networks. As a result, they can provide information to schools which is vital in meeting special educational needs, and may in addition help to promote liaison with homes and the local community. The need for effective collaboration between educational and social services has been recognized for many years and the 1989 Children Act provides a framework in relation to children deemed 'in need'. This category includes many children with special educational needs, for its definition embraces those who are 'unlikely to achieve or maintain … a reasonable standard of health or development … physical, intellectual, emotional, social or behavioural' without the provision of specified services, and those who have significant permanent disabilities. A major principle of the Act is that schools and other agencies must work together in close cooperation, and must involve both children and their parents in decisions about the services they provide. Social services departments have a responsibility to inform and consult with LEAs if they have any concerns about the educational welfare of a child. They also have duties to contribute to the provision of services for that child: for example, by providing care or supervised activities outside school hours and during the school holidays. Similarly, LEAs should inform social services departments of their concerns so that, where appropriate, assessments of educational need under the 1996 Education Act can be coordinated with assessments of wider aspects of need. The whole emphasis of the legislation is that the extent to which any individual child's difficulties hinder his or her development depends not only on the severity of that difficulty but also on the support provided at home, in school, and by the various support agencies.

Health authority support

The health visitor service provides an important source of support for families and pre-school children at home. Health visitors screen vision, hearing and language development and can alert other services to any indications of particular need. Some have specialized training which equips them to offer direct help to children with specific developmental difficulties or delays and their parents. When children are of school age, school doctors and nurses represent the main source of advice and support on health-related issues and may play an important role in assessing special educational need. In addition to routine screenings and general advice on health education, they will monitor the health of particular pupils, identifying any sources of difficulty and advising on the educational implications of these.

Outside the school context, individual pupils with special educational needs may have contact with a wide range of medical specialists, such as paediatricians, orthopaedic surgeons, neurologists, vision and hearing specialists, and so on. Those with significant emotional and/or behavioural disturbance may be involved with multidisciplinary child guidance teams, jointly run by the health and education services, and here there is a clear need for close liaison with school staff. This is equally the case when pupils are receiving support from physiotherapists or speech and language therapists. These therapists typically work in hospitals, clinics and special school settings, although speech and language therapy and, more rarely, physiotherapy may sometimes be provided in ordinary schools. They are particularly concerned with the assessment and diagnosis of motor or communication difficulties, programme development and the monitoring of individual progress. In addition to their direct involvement with children, they usually work closely with their parents. It is crucial that they also liaise with their teachers, for they can provide specialist advice on appropriate methods to extend specific skills, as well as information on resources and strategies which can facilitate the children's access to the curriculum.

Inter-agency collaboration

There has been a long-standing consensus of opinion that collaboration between the education, social and health services and also with voluntary agencies is essential for effective special educational provision. However, it should be acknowledged that it has often proved difficult to achieve this. Davie (1993) and Dessent (1996) have outlined the range of obstacles that impede inter-agency collaboration. These lie particularly within their separate professional development and administrative systems and in the discrete legal frameworks that govern their operation. Current initiatives to strengthen links between governmental departments responsible for education and health may help to alleviate some of the chronic problems that have been experienced in clarifying roles and responsibilities, for example in relation to the resourcing of speech and language therapy. Nevertheless, it is evident that effective interdisciplinary involvement for children and families will continue to depend on the quality of the working relationship that individual professionals can establish jointly together. Positive relationships between those working in different professional disciplines require mutual recognition and valuing of the contribution each has to make.

Reciprocal systems of support

Although the emphasis in this chapter so far has been placed on the way in which particular colleagues can advise and support teachers to help them meet pupils' needs, it is important to stress that this should not be seen as a one-way process. From their day-to-day interactions with pupils, and from their continuous assessment and monitoring of the effectiveness of different classroom strategies, class teachers gather insights and information which are invaluable to other professionals. If support systems are to be successful in assisting both the pupils and all the staff who work with them, it is essential that the working relationships that this entails are characterized by mutual understanding and respect for the skills, knowledge and expertise that all have to offer. This necessitates an explicit recognition of the complementary roles of all those involved, and of the need for reciprocal support. Furthermore, these perspectives do not only apply to professional networks but are of equal importance when considering the contribution of parents to their children's education.

Parental support for their children's learning

It has been implicit throughout this book that it is vital that teachers should consult with parents and involve them as fully as possible in their children's education. It is necessary, therefore, in this concluding section, to look more explicitly at the question of why parental involvement should merit such an emphasis.

In principle, the importance for schools of seeking to promote positive home–school relationships has long been acknowledged. Since the 1960s a number of governmental reports have addressed the issue, and it was a central theme of the Warnock Committee's recommendations on special educational provision. In a chapter entitled 'Parents as partners' it asserted that:

> the successful education of children with special educational needs is dependent on the full involvement of their parents: indeed, unless the parents are seen as equal partners in the educational process the purpose of our report will be frustrated.
>
> (DES 1978: para. 9.1)

Throughout the educational legislation of the 1980s and 1990s, prevalent political themes of consumerism and the accountability of services found expression in the continued strengthening of parental rights in relation to their children's schooling. These rights, which were summarized in the updated Parent's Charter (DfE 1994d), include access to detailed information about their own child's progress and attainments as well as about whole school policies and practices. For those parents whose children have a statement of special educational need, further rights include involvement in statutory assessment procedures and in subsequent annual reviews. While home–school liaison is seen as important for all children, it is generally recognized as even more essential where children have special educational need. Thus, the arguments which were stated in the Warnock Report were reiterated and reinforced in the Code of Practice (DfE 1994a), which identifies partnership with parents as one of the 'fundamental principles' which should govern special educational provision. The Code elaborates the rationale for this as follows:

> The relationship between parents of children with special educational needs and the school which their child is attending has a crucial bearing on the child's educational progress and the effectiveness of any school-based action … [School-based action should] take account of the wishes, feelings and knowledge of parents at all stages. Children's progress will be diminished if their parents are not seen as partners in the educational process with unique knowledge and information to impart. Professional help can seldom be wholly effective unless it builds upon parents' capacity to be involved and unless parents consider that professionals take account of what they say and treat their views and anxieties as intrinsically important.
>
> (DfE 1994a: para. 2:28)

This rationale is based on the premise that parents and teachers have complementary skills, knowledge and experiences to bring to children's learning, and that educational progress may best be achieved by actively acknowledging and respecting these. Through the very nature of their role, parents acquire unique knowledge and experience of their own children, and exert a significant influence on all aspects of their development. An extensive body of research literature has described the way in which, from their earliest inter-actions, parents provide the sorts of stimulation that lay the foundations for subsequent social, emotional, physical and intellec-tual growth. While many parents may not view their role as one which incorporates systematic teaching, it is evident that a great deal of natural teaching goes on at home before a child starts school. There is no reason to assume that this ceases once formal education begins. Rather, a number of studies (e.g. Tizard *et al.* 1988) have demonstrated that a large proportion of parents also adopt more explicit teaching aims during the primary school years, particularly in relation to literacy and numeracy skills. Perhaps surprisingly, given the weight that has always been attributed to homework during secondary school, there is little comparable information on general patterns of parental support for older children. Common sense would suggest that any direct assistance will vary with their children's growing independence as well as with parents' confi-dence in their own competence to help. However, it seems clear that less direct forms of parental support are likely to remain as a signifi-cant influence on learning throughout a child's schooling.

Schools, however, are not always aware of the nature of the help that parents provide at home. Moreover, it is not unusual to find that the contributions of particular parents to their children's educa-tion are judged by teachers to be inappropriate, inadequate or deficient in some way. Thus, as Croll and Moses (1985) found, chil-dren's learning or behavioural difficulties at school are frequently ascribed in part, if not primarily, to their home circumstances. Where this is so, too often parents may be more readily viewed by schools as 'part of the problem', rather than as a potential source of support in promoting their children's progress.

It is worth considering the evidence upon which such judge-ments are based. As previously discussed, it has been acknowledged for some time that children from 'lower-working-class' backgrounds typically do less well at school, and are more likely to be identified by their teachers as having moderate learning or emotional and behavioural difficulties. Comparative studies of early parent–child interactions have looked for possible explanations in the children's home experiences. Thus, for example, social class differences have been sought and found in child-rearing strategies such as style of language use and attitudes to discipline and control. There is no doubt that a 'child-centred' approach at home is made easier by comfortable material and physical circumstances, and that poverty and oppressive home conditions can have a significant influence on patterns of family interaction. However, it is important to draw attention to the significant work of Tizard and Hughes (1984) and Wells and his colleagues (Wells 1983) in this area. These researchers, while not denying differences between families of different socio-economic status, have described the richness of children's stimulation at home among 'working-class' families. In doing so they provide evidence that seriously challenges the notion that those children suffer from linguistic or cognitive deprivation outside school.

The differences in experience that children bring with them when they start school may, however, have a lasting impact on their attainments and behaviour. While one might hope that schools could in some way 'compensate' for assumed or real disadvantage at home, the evidence suggests that this does not often happen. Rather, a number of studies report that, even where children of different social class backgrounds enter school with similar levels of attainment, those from families of the lowest socio-economic status tend to make poorer progress (Mortimore and Blackstone 1982). One explanation for this that is commonly offered is that their parents demonstrate less interest in their education. Undeniably, parental interest, support and encouragement of learning can be crucial factors in children's progress at school. However, it must be emphasized that there is little evidence to suggest that this is notably lacking among any particular social group as a whole. Some parents are diffident or lack confidence about what they can contribute to their child's formal education. Others feel apprehensive in their dealings with schools and the authority that teachers represent. This can frequently be the case for those whose own earlier experiences as pupils at school were poor, and for those whose current contacts are dominated by discussion of the problems rather than the positive achievements of their children. It is important that any such feelings of apprehension are not misjudged as a lack of interest. Unless a school takes active steps to reach out to all parents and to communicate a genuine respect both for their children and themselves, it is unlikely that the full benefits of parental support will be felt.

Although the influence of home and family on children's learning should not be underestimated, neither should that of school. Research into school effectiveness demonstrates that even where the entry skills and home backgrounds of pupils are similar, schools can vary in the standards of educational attainment and behaviour that they achieve. It is evident too that teachers' expectations, the way in which they categorize pupils, their classroom interactions and teaching style can all affect children's learning progress. Some studies have suggested that social class assumptions play a part in the judgements that are made about children at school. That is, teachers may hold different expectations of children from different social groups and home backgrounds. It is perhaps inevitable that their assessments will be influenced by the cultural norms with which they are most familiar, but it has frequently been argued that the 'cultural loading' of schools generally favours certain social groups more than others. Certainly, while a 'gap' can be described between the expectations and demands of home and school for all children (e.g. Tizard and Hughes 1984), it is wider for some than for others. Just how far the gap should be bridged is open to debate, but at the very least it seems essential that teachers should not make assumptions about their pupils' home backgrounds. In order to avoid this, teachers require accurate information and insights into children's learning experiences outside school. The implication, therefore, is that teachers need to seek ways to establish effective methods of communication with pupils' parents.

Constructive two-way communication between home and school has been identified as one of the factors associated with effective education at both primary and secondary levels (Reynolds and Cuttance 1992). If good parent–teacher relationships are to be established, this requires positive attitudes from staff and a considerable whole school commitment to the time and effort that may be involved. Given the pressures of competing priorities in schools, therefore, it is important to explore the evidence for the view that parents might be willing to become involved more closely in their children's education and, furthermore, that this would lead to enhanced progress.

In the pre-school years, if their children have significantly delayed development, it is frequently reported that most parents wish for practical guidance and support on how they might best promote their children's learning (Dale 1996). This is fortunate from a professional point of view, because research into early intervention schemes suggests that their effectiveness is likely to be sustained and enhanced where parents are actively involved. Accordingly, parental involvement is usually now seen as an essential component of such schemes. Over the last twenty years, a home-based service which relies on parents as the primary teachers of their children has become a predominant form of early provision for children with special educational needs. This service is based on the Portage model (White and Cameron 1987). The exact form it takes can vary from authority to authority, but where it has been evaluated there is evidence that both children and parents benefit from their involvement (White 1997). It seems probable that many parents who have experienced a Portage service will seek to continue their teaching role in some way once their children begin school. In recognition of this, some authorities have extended their schemes into primary schools, where parents and teachers work together on individual educational programmes.

For most parents, however, their children's special educational needs are only identified at some stage during formal schooling. Their readiness to work together with the school will clearly be influenced not only by their existing relationship with the staff, but also by the manner in which they are alerted to the causes for concern. Where the parents' perception is that their views are not listened to, that their own assessment of their child's needs is judged less valid than those of the teachers, or that they are implicitly criticized, it is not surprising if they are unenthusiastic. On the other hand, if teachers are open and demonstrate that they value the parents' perspectives and insights, and respect the contribution they make to support their child's learning, one might predict a more positive response. Certainly, the evidence from well-planned schemes to involve parents in the teaching of reading suggests that there is a great deal of willingness among parents to work with teachers to help their children.

Most children with special educational needs experience difficulties in their reading, and it is in this area of the curriculum that there is the most powerful evidence for the benefits of parent–teacher collaboration. Hewison and her colleagues found that among children from working-class backgrounds, levels of reading attainment were strongly associated with whether their mothers regularly listened to them reading at home (Hewison and Tizard 1980). On the basis of this finding, they initiated a major intervention study known as the Haringey project, which aimed to explore whether it could be demonstrated that such parental help led to enhanced achievements for their children. Parents of 6-year-old children were asked to hear their children read on a regular basis over a two-year period. Most not only agreed to do so, but also maintained a high level of commitment to the project throughout the two years. Their children's reading attainments were monitored and compared with those of two other groups of pupils. The first of these were given regular input at school by a specialist teacher of reading. The second received no additional help other than that which was normally provided by their class teachers. The results showed that children in the parental involvement group made significant and lasting gains in comparison with the others. Additionally, teachers and parents spoke of wider benefits to the children's progress at school, and of their satisfaction with the improved home–school relationships which had been developed (Tizard *et al.* 1982).

Not surprisingly, this study gave a considerable impetus to other schemes which sought to promote parental involvement in reading. A wide variety of approaches have been adopted and, while not all have been rigorously evaluated, gains have been described both in children's reading skills and also in their general approach to learning and behaviour at school (Topping and Wolfendale 1985). Increasingly, therefore, as schools become more convinced of the benefits, and more confident in their approach, parental involvement schemes have been developed in a number of different ways. They have widened their focus to incorporate pre-school (Hannon 1995) and family literacy (Wolfendale and Topping 1995), other aspects of the formal curriculum such as mathematics (Merttens and Vass 1993), and broader concerns such as behaviour management (e.g. Miller 1994). The extent of planned and active parental involvement varies in different areas of the country, and is more associated with primary than secondary education. However, over the last decade there has been an evident growth of these schemes in all sectors of the school system (Jowett *et al.* 1991). Some are focused specifically on children with special educational needs, particularly at secondary level, but an underlying principle during the earlier years of school is that many potential areas of difficulty might be prevented if parents can be fully involved.

There is, then, a strong educational rationale for promoting positive approaches to parent–teacher collaboration. However, it should be noted that the parental involvement schemes described above do not necessarily represent the type of partnership between home and school envisaged in the Warnock Report and the Code of Practice. Typically, parents are involved on the school's terms, and there may be little explicit attempt to take their priorities and perspectives into account when developing the approach that is followed. Thus, it is quite possible for teachers to participate in a scheme without acknowledging the skills, knowledge and insights that parents might contribute. Furthermore, if active collaboration of this kind is seen as the major way in which parents can be involved in their children's education, this can distract attention from those who are unable or unwilling to take part. There is no doubt that where parents and teachers work together with a positive focus on children's learning and development this can do much to enhance home–school relationships. However, if these relationships are to be established on a basis of mutual trust and respect, there is a need for a flexible system of genuine two-way communication which goes far wider than only asking parents to take part in programmes of work designed by the school.

In both the Warnock Report and the Code of Practice, parents and teachers are described as having complementary contributions to make to children's development and learning, and what Wolfendale (1988) has referred to as 'equivalent expertise'. The term 'partnership' is used to characterize a relationship in which there is a full sharing of the unique expertise parents have in relation to their own children with the wider educational expertise of teachers and other professionals. The Code is explicit that parents must be seen as key participants in assessment and decision-making about provision to meet their children's educational needs, as well as in the review process. Schools therefore need to consider the information they provide, their accessibility and their arrangements for promoting working partnerships with parents (DfE 1994a: para. 2:33). Taking each of these in turn, first, parents must be provided with clear and accurate information about the school's SEN policy, the support which will be available for their child and the ways in which they can expect to be consulted and involved in the educational process. Second, schools should look at ways of making themselves as approachable as possible, so that the information they provide is accessible and readily understood, and that parents feel neither inhibited nor anxious about making contact with staff. Third, there need to be procedures in place for encouraging, recording and responding to parental views, so that the special educational provision which is made is fully informed by dialogue with pupils' parents. The requirement that staff should aim for active parental involvement throughout an ongoing cycle of assessment, decision-making and review poses considerable challenges for schools. If this is to be achieved within a spirit of partnership then positive attitudes on all sides are clearly fundamental. Schools can do a great deal to promote these. A necessary starting point is an agreed whole school policy which supports home–school liaison together with staff development practices which promote both constructive attitudes and also the skills, knowledge and understanding that teachers require to work successfully with parents.

Partnership has frequently been described as an ideal rather than an attainable goal. Certainly, as Sandow and her colleagues (1987) observed, it is a term far more readily used by professionals than parents when referring to home–school interactions. Nevertheless, there is no doubt that it is a goal for which it is worth striving. Parents represent a potentially very powerful resource in the education of all children. The greater the level of a child's educational need, the more important it is that all available resources are brought together in order to meet this. There are strong grounds for the argument that special educational needs can best be met where teachers and parents aim to establish a relationship of reciprocal support.

Discussion points

1   Extra support in school for pupils with special educational needs is most effective where it is based on joint planning between class teacher and support teacher. In order to explore

why this might be so, consider: (i) the knowledge and skills that class teachers can contribute to joint planning; and (ii) the ways in which they might best draw on specialist help to support their own approach to meeting pupils' needs.

2 Discuss the areas of overlap and the boundaries between the roles and responsibilities of parents and teachers in children's education. To what extent can their roles be seen as complementary?

3 What would you see as the main rationale for home–school partnership? Consider the challenges that the notion of partnership presents for teachers, and the extent to which it might be viewed as an achievable goal.

Further reading

Hornby, G. (1995) *Working with Parents of Children with Special Needs*, London: Cassell.

Lacey, P. and Lomas, J. (1993) *Support Services and the Curriculum*, London: David Fulton.

Wolfendale, S. (ed.) (1997) *Working with Parents of SEN Children after the Code of Practice*, London: David Fulton.

Sources of further information

Related to the full range of special educational needs

The National Association for Special Educational Needs (NASEN), NASEN House, 4/5 Amber Business Village, Amber Close, Amington, Tamworth B77 4RP. This association, which was formed by the amalgamation of two former organizations (NCSE and NARE), publishes two journals concerning educational provision for pupils with special educational needs: the *British Journal of Special Education* and *Support for Learning: British Journal of Learning Support*.

An independent magazine, *Special Children*, which is aimed at parents, teachers and others concerned with special educational needs, is based at 73 All Saints Road, Kings Heath, Birmingham B14 7LN.

Publications and information sheets regarding inclusive education are produced by the Centre for Studies on Inclusive Education (CSIE), at 1 Redland Close, Elm Lane, Redland, Bristol BS6 6UE.

Related to specific forms of special educational needs

There are many voluntary organizations that bring together children, parents and professionals with a specific focus on a particular form of special educational need. The following selective list, in alphabetical order, draws attention to some of those that can provide information and guidance for teachers.

AFASIC (The Association for All Speech Impaired Children), 347 Central Markets, Smithfield, London EClA 9NH.

Association for Spina Bifida and Hydrocephalus, 42 Park Road, Peterborough PEl 2UQ.

British Dyslexia Association, 98 London Road, Reading RG1 5AU.

Down's Syndrome Association, 155 Mitcham Road, London SW17 9PG.

In Touch, 10 Norman Road, Sale, M33 3DF. (Provides a newsletter with information and contacts, particularly for parents of children with rare or complex impairments.)

MENCAP (The Royal Society for Mentally Handicapped Children and Adults), 123 Golden Lane, London EC1Y 0RT.

National Autistic Society, 276 Willesden Lane, London NW2 5RB.

National Deaf Children's Society, 45 Hereford Road, London W2 5AH.

RNIB (The Royal National Institute for the Blind), 224 Great Portland Street, London W1N 6AA.

RNID (The Royal National Institute for the Deaf), 105 Gower Street, London WC1 6AH.

SCOPE, 12 Park Crescent, London W1N 4EQ. (Society concerned with the needs of children with cerebral palsy and their families.)

References

Ainscow, M. (1989) 'How should we respond to individual needs?', in M. Ainscow and A. Florek (eds) *Special Educational Needs: Towards a Whole School Approach*, London: David Fulton.

——(ed.) (1991) *Effective Schools for All*, London: David Fulton.

——(1995a) 'Education for all: making it happen', *Support for Learning* 10, 4, 147–55.

——(1995b) 'Special needs through school improvement; school improvement through special needs', in C. Clark, A. Dyson and A. Millward (eds) *Towards Inclusive Schools?*, London: David Fulton.

Ainscow, M. and Muncey, J. (1989) *Meeting Individual Needs*, London: David Fulton.

Ainscow, M. and Tweddle, D. (1979) *Preventing Classroom Failure: An Objective Approach*, London: Wiley.

——(1984) *Early Learning Skills Analysis*, London: Wiley.

——(1988) *Encouraging Classroom Success*, London: David Fulton.

Anwyll, S. (1998) 'Main principles and rationale of the Literacy Hour', paper given at NASEN conference, The Literacy Hour and Special Educational Needs, Sheffield, 17 October 1998.

Audit Commission / HMI (1992) *Getting in on the Act: provision for pupils with special educational needs*, London: HMSO.

Balshaw, M. (1991) *Help in the Classroom*, London: David Fulton.

Barnes, D. (1982) *Practical Curriculum Study*, London: Routledge & Kegan Paul.

Barton, L. (1995) 'The politics of education for all', *Support for Learning* 10, 4, 156–60.

Beveridge, S. (1997) 'Implementing partnership with parents in schools', in S. Wolfendale (ed.) *Working with Parents of SEN Children after the Code of Practice*, London: David Fulton.

Bishop, J. and Gregory, S. (1986) 'Hearing impairment', in B. Gillham (ed.) *Handicapping Conditions in Childhood*, London: Croom Helm.

Blunkett, D. (1997) Editorial, *British Journal of Special Education* 24, 4, 150–1.

Bolton, A. (1997) *Losing the Thread: Pupils' and Parents' Voices about Education for Sick Children*, London: NAESC.

Booth, T. (1998) 'The poverty of special education: theories to the rescue?', in C. Clark, A. Dyson and A. Millward (eds) *Theorising Special Education*, London: Routledge.

Bowers, T., Dee, L. and West, M. (1998) 'The Code in action: some school perceptions of its user-friendliness', *Support for Learning* 13, 3, 99–104.

Brennan, W. K. (1985) *Curriculum for Special Needs*, Milton Keynes: Open University Press.

Buckley, S., Bird, G. and Byrne, A. (1996) 'Reading acquisition by young children', in B. Stratford and P. Gunn (eds) *New Approaches to Down Syndrome*, London: Cassell.

Clark, C., Dyson, A. and Millward, A. (eds) (1995) *Towards Inclusive Schools?*, London: David Fulton.

——(eds) (1998) *Theorising Special Education*, London: Routledge.

Clark, C., Dyson, A., Millward, A. and Skidmore, D. (1997) *New Directions in Special Needs: Innovations in Mainstream Schools*, London: Cassell.

Cole, T. (1989) *Apart or A Part? Integration and the Growth of British Special Education*, Milton Keynes: Open University Press.

Coltheart, M. and Jackson, E. (1998) 'Defining dyslexia', *Child Psychology and Psychiatry Review* 3, 1, 12–16.

Cooper, P. and Ideus, K. (eds) (1995) *Attention Deficit/Hyperactivity Disorder: Educational, Medical and Cultural Issues*, East Sutton: AWCEBD.

Cooper, P., Smith, C. and Upton, G. (1994) *Emotional and Behavioural Difficulties: From Theory to Practice*, London: Routledge.

Croll, P. and Moses, D. (1985) *One in Five: The Assessment and Incidence of Special Educational Needs*, London: Routledge & Kegan Paul.

Dale, N. (1996) *Working with Families of Children with Special Needs*, London: Routledge.

Daniels, H., Hey, V., Leonard, D. and Smith, M. (1996) *Gender and Special Needs in Mainstream Schooling*, ESRC Report R000235059, Birmingham: University of Birmingham.

Davie, R. (1993) 'Implementing Warnock's multiprofessional approach', in J. Visser and G. Upton (eds) *Special Education in Britain after Warnock*, London: David Fulton.

——(1996) 'Raising the achievements of pupils with special educational needs', *Support for Learning* 11, 2, 51–6.

DES (1978) *Special Educational Needs* (The Warnock Report), Cmnd 7212, London: HMSO.

——(1981) *Education Act (1981)*, London: HMSO.

——(1988) *Education Reform Act (1988)*, London: HMSO.

——(1989) *Discipline in Schools* (The Elton Report), London: HMSO.

Dessent, T. (1987) *Making the Ordinary School Special*, Lewes: Falmer Press.

——(1996) *Meeting Special Educational Needs: Options for Partnership between Health, Social and Educational Services*, Tamworth: NASEN.

DfE (1993) *Education Act (1993)*, London: HMSO.

——(1994a) *The Code of Practice on the Identification and Assessment of Special Educational Needs*, London: HMSO.

——(1994b) *The Education (SEN) (Information) Regulations*, London: HMSO.

——(1994c) *The Organisation of Special Educational Provision*, Circular Number 6/94, London: HMSO.

——(1994d) *Our Children's Education: The Updated Parent's Charter*, London: HMSO.

——(1995) *The National Curriculum*, London: HMSO.

DfEE (1996a) *The Education Act (1996)*, London: HMSO.

——(1996b) *Supporting Pupils with Medical Needs in School*, Circular Number 14/96, London: HMSO.

——(1997a) *Excellence for All Children: Meeting Special Educational Needs*, London: HMSO.

——(1997b) *The SENCO Guide*, London: DfEE.

——(1998a) *Meeting Special Educational Needs: A Programme of Action*, London: DfEE.

——(1998b) *The National Literacy Project*, London: HMSO.

Diamond, C. (1993) 'A reconsideration of the role of SEN support services: will they get in on the Act?', *Support for Learning* 8, 3, 91–8.

Docking, J. (1989) 'The Good Behaviour Guide: HMI observations on school discipline', in N. Jones (ed.) *Special Educational Needs Review*, vol. 1, Lewes: Falmer Press.

Dyson, A. (1997) 'Social and educational disadvantage: reconnecting special needs education', *British Journal of Special Education* 24, 4, 152–7.

Dyson, A. and Gains, K. (1995) 'The role of the special needs coordinator: poisoned chalice or crock of gold?', *Support for Learning* 10, 2, 50–6.

Farrell, M. (1998) 'Notes on the Green Paper: an initial response', *British Journal of Special Education* 25, 1, 13–15.

Farrell, P. (1997) *Teaching Children with Learning Difficulties*, London: Cassell.

Fontana, D. (1985) *Classroom Control: Understanding and Guiding Classroom Behaviour*, London: BPS/Methuen.

Foot, H. C., Morgan, M. J. and Shute, R. H. (eds) (1990) *Children Helping Children*, Chichester: John Wiley and Sons.

Friel, J. (1997) *Children with Special Needs: Assessment, Law and Practice: Caught in the Act*, 4th edn, London: Jessica Kingsley.

Frith, U. (1989) *Autism*, Oxford: Blackwell.

Galloway, D. (1985) *Schools, Pupils and Special Educational Needs*, London: Croom Helm.

——(1990) *Pupil Welfare and Counselling*, Harlow: Longman.

Galvin, P. (1989) 'Behaviour problems and cognitive processes', in D. A. Sugden (ed.) *Cognitive Approaches in Special Education*, Lewes: Falmer Press.

Galvin, P., Mercer, S. and Costa, P. (1990) *Building a Better Behaved School*, Harlow: Longman.

Garner, P. (1993) 'Exclusions: the challenge to schools', *Support for Learning* 8, 3, 99–103.

——(1994) 'Exclusions from schools', *Pastoral Care* 12, 3–10.

Goacher, B., Evans, J., Welton, J. and Wedell, K. (1988) *Policy and Provision for Special Educational Needs: Implementing the 1981 Education Act*, London: Cassell.

Goddard, A. (1983) 'Processes in special education', in G. Blenkin and V. Kelly (eds) *The Primary Curriculum in Action*, London: Harper & Row.

——(1997) 'The role of individual educational plans/programmes in special education: a critique', *Support for Learning* 12, 4, 170–4.

Gregory, S., Knight, P., McCracken, W., Powers, S. and Watson, L. (eds) (1998) *Issues in Deaf Education*, London: David Fulton.

Gross, J. (1996) 'The weight of the evidence: parental advocacy and resource allocation to children with statements of special educational need', *Support for Learning* 11, 1, 3–8.

Hannon, P. (1995) *Literacy, Home and School: Research and Practice in Teaching Literacy with Parents*, London: Falmer Press.

Hart, S. (1996) *Beyond Special Needs*, London: Paul Chapman Publishing.

——(1998) 'Paperwork or practice? Shifting the emphasis of the Code towards teaching, learning and inclusion', *Support for Learning* 13, 2, 76–81.

Hawkridge, D. and Vincent, T. (1992) *Learning Difficulties and Computers: Access to the Curriculum*, London: Jessica Kingsley.

Hegarty, S. (1993) 'Reviewing the literature on integration', *European Journal of Special Needs Education* 8, 3, 194–200.

Hegarty, S., Pocklington, K. and Lucas, D. (1981) *Educating Pupils with Special Needs in the Ordinary School*, Windsor: NFER-Nelson.

Henderson, S. and Sugden, D. (1991) 'Pupils with motor impairment', in National Children's Bureau *Signposts to Special Needs*, Nottingham: NES Arnold.

Hewison, J. and Tizard, J. (1980) 'Parental involvement and reading attainment', *British Journal of Educational Psychology* 50, 209–15.

HMI (1989) *A Survey of Pupils with Special Educational Needs in Ordinary Schools 1988–1989*, London: DES.

——(1990) *Education Observed: Special Needs Issues*, London: HMSO.

——(1991) *National Curriculum and Special Needs*, London: DES.

Hodgson, A. (1989) 'Meeting special needs in mainstream classrooms', in M. Ainscow and A. Florek (eds) *Special Educational Needs: Towards a Whole School Approach*, London: David Fulton.

Hornby, G. (1995) *Working with Parents of Children with Special Needs*, London: Cassell.

Hornby, G., Davies, G. and Taylor, G. (1995) *The Special Educational Needs Coordinator's Handbook*, London: Routledge.

House of Commons Select Committee (1987) *Special Educational Needs: Implementation of the 1981 Education Act*, London: HMSO.

ILEA (1985) *Educational Opportunities for All?* (The Fish Report), London: ILEA.

Jones, K. and Charlton, T. (eds) (1996) *Overcoming Learning and Behaviour Difficulties: Partnership with Pupils*, London: Routledge.

Jones, N. J. (1983) 'An integrative approach to special educational needs', *Forum* 25, 2, 36–9.

Jordan, R. R. and Powell, S. D. (1995) *Understanding and Teaching Children with Autism*, Chichester: Wiley.

Jowett, S., Baginsky, M. and McNeill, M. M. (1991) *Building Bridges: Parental Involvement in Schools*, Windsor: NFER-Nelson.

Jowett, S., Hegarty, S. and Moses, D. (1988) *Joining Forces: A Study of Links between Special and Ordinary Schools*, Windsor: NFER-Nelson.

Lacey, P. and Lomas, J. (1993) *Support Services and the Curriculum*, London: David Fulton.

Leach, D. J. and Raybould, E. C. (1977) *Learning and Behaviour Difficulties in School*, London: Open Books.

Lee, B. and Henkhuzens, Z. (1996) *Integration in Progress: Pupils with Special Needs in Mainstream Schools*, Slough: NFER.

Lewis, A. (1995a) *Special Needs Provision in Mainstream Primary Schools*, Stoke on Trent: Trentham.

——(1995b) *Primary Special Needs and the National Curriculum*, 2nd edn, London: Routledge.

——(1996) 'Summative National Curriculum assessment of primary aged children with special needs', *British Journal of Special Education*, 23, 1, 9–14.

Lewis, A., Neill, S. and Campbell, J. (1996) '"It doesn't concern us!" The Code of Practice and its relevance for special schools, units and services', *British Journal of Special Education* 23, 3, 105–9.

——(1997) 'SENCOs and the Code: a national survey', *Support for Learning* 12, 1, 3–9.

Lorenz, S. (1996) *Supporting Support Assistants*, Bury: Bury Professional Development Centre.

Loxley, A. and Bines, H. (1995) 'Implementing the Code of Practice: professional responses', *Support for Learning* 10, 4, 185–9.

Lunt, I. (1990) 'Local management of schools and education', in H. Daniels and J. Ware (eds) *Special Educational Needs and the National Curriculum*, Bedford Way Series, London: Kogan Page.

——(1998) 'A chance for change?', *Special*, Summer, 24–5.

Martin, D. and Miller, C. (1995) *Speech and Language Difficulties in the Classroom*, London: David Fulton.

Mason, H. (1995) *Spotlight on Special Educational Needs: Visual Impairment*, Tamworth: NASEN.

Merttens, R. and Vass, J. (eds) (1993) *Partnerships in Maths: Parents and Schools*, Lewes: Falmer Press.

Miller, A. (1994) 'Parents and difficult behaviour: always the problem or part of the solution?', in P. Gray, A. Miller and J. Noakes (eds) *Challenging Behaviour in Schools*, London: Routledge.

Montgomery, D. (1989) *Managing Behaviour Problems*, London: Hodder & Stoughton.

Mortimore, J. and Blackstone, T. (1982) *Disadvantage and Education*, London: Heinemann.

Mortimore, P., Sammons, P., Stoll, L., Lewis, D. and Ecob, R. (1988) *School Matters*, London: Open Books.

Mosley, J. (1993) *Turn Round Your School*, Wisbech: LDA.

Moss, H. and Reason, R. (1998) 'Interactive group work with young children needing additional help in learning to read', *Support for Learning* 13, 1, 32–8.

NCC (1989a) *Implementing the National Curriculum: Participation by Pupils with Special Educational Needs*, Circular no. 5, York: NCC.

——(1989b) *Curriculum Guidance 2: A Curriculum for All*, York: NCC.

Norwich, B. (1990) *Reappraising Special Needs Education*, London: Cassell.

——(1994) *Segregation and Inclusion: English LEA Statistics*, Bristol: CSIE.

——(1996) 'Special needs education or education for all: connective specialisation and ideological impurity', *British Journal of Special Education* 23, 3, 100–4.

——(1998) 'The future of SEN policy and practice after the White and Green Papers', paper presented at the Centre for Policy Studies in Education Seminar, University of Leeds, 4 June 1998.

OFSTED (1996) *The Implementation of the Code of Practice for Pupils with Special Educational Needs*, London: HMSO.

Parsons, C. and Howlett, K. (1996) 'Permanent exclusions from school: a case where society is failing its children', *Support for Learning* 11, 3, 109–12.

Pollard, A. (1988) 'The social context of special needs in classrooms', in G. Thomas and A. Feiler (eds) *Planning for Special Needs: A Whole School Approach*, Oxford: Blackwell.

Putnam, J. W. (1993) 'The process of cooperative learning', in J. W. Putnam (ed.) *Cooperative Learning and Strategies for Inclusion*, Baltimore: Paul H. Brookes Publishing Co.

Reason, R. (1998) 'Interactive approaches to developing phonics', paper given at NASEN conference, The Literacy Hour and Special Educational Needs, Sheffield, 17 October 1998.

Reynolds, D. (1995) 'Using school effectiveness knowledge for children with special needs – the problems and possibilities', in C. Clark, A. Dyson and A. Millward (eds) *Towards Inclusive Schools?*, London: David Fulton.

Reynolds, D. and Cuttance, P. (eds) (1992) *School Effectiveness: Research, Policy and Practice*, London: Cassell.

Roaf, C. (1989) 'Developing whole school policy: a secondary school perspective', in C. Roaf and H. Bines (eds) *Needs, Rights and Opportunities: Developing Approaches to Special Education*, Lewes: Falmer Press.

Roaf, C. and Bines, H. (eds) (1989) *Needs, Rights and Opportunities: Developing Approaches to Special Education*, Lewes: Falmer Press.

Rogers, W. (1994) *Behaviour Recovery*, London: Longman.

Rose, R. (1991) 'A jigsaw approach to group work', *British Journal of Special Education* 18, 2, 54–8.

Rouse, M. and Agbenu, R. (1998) 'Assessment and special educational needs: teachers' dilemmas', *British Journal of Special Education* 25, 2, 81–7.

Russell, P. (1996) 'Partnership with parents', proceedings of the DfEE conference, The Code of Practice Two Years On, London and York, 26 September and 2 October 1996.

——(1997) 'Parents as partners: some early impressions of the impact of the Code of Practice', in S. Wolfendale (ed.) *Working with Parents of SEN Children after the Code of Practice*, London: David Fulton.

Rutter, M., Maugham, B., Mortimore, P., Ouston, J. and Smith, A. (1979) *Fifteen Thousand Hours: Secondary Schools and Their Effects on Pupils*, London: Open Books.

Sammons, P. and Mortimore, P. (1990) 'Pupil achievements and pupil alienation in junior school', in J. Docking (ed.) *Education and Alienation in the Junior School*, Basingstoke: Falmer Press.

Sandow, S., Stafford, D. and Stafford, P. (1987) *An Agreed Understanding? Parent-professional Communication and the 1981 Education Act*, Windsor: NFER-Nelson.

Sewell, G. (1996) *Special Needs Provision: Assessment, Concern and Action*, London: Cassell.

Simmons, K. (1996) 'In defence of entitlement', *Support for Learning* 11, 3, 105–8.

——(1998) 'Rights at risk', *British Journal of Special Education* 25, 1, 9–12.

Slavin, R. E. (1990) *Cooperative Learning: Theory, Research and Practice*, Englewood Cliffs, NJ: Prentice-Hall.

Smith, C. and Laslett, R. (1993) *Effective Classroom Management*, 2nd edn, London: Routledge.

Solity, J. and Bull, S. (1987) *Special Needs: Bridging the Curriculum Gap*, Milton Keynes: Open University Press.

Stakes, R. and Hornby, G. (1997) *Change in Special Education*, London: Cassell.

Stenhouse, L. (1975) *An Introduction to Curriculum Research and Development*, London: Heinemann.

Stratford, B. and Gunn, P. (eds) (1996) *New Approaches to Down's Syndrome*, London: Cassell.

Sugden, D., Beveridge, S., Burns, J., Drizi, A., Rose, C. and Shepherd, M. (1989) *Leeds Education Authority Special Educational Needs Support Programme in Middle and High Schools: Evaluation Report 1*, Leeds: University of Leeds Press.

Sugden, D. A. and Wright, H. (1998) *Motor Coordination Disorders in Children*, Thousand Oaks, CA: Sage Publications.

Swann, W. (1988a) 'Integration? Look twice at statistics', *British Journal of Special Education* 15, 102.

——(1988b) 'Learning difficulties and curriculum reform: integration or differentiation?', in G. Thomas and A. Feiler (eds) *Planning for Special Needs: A Whole School Approach*, Oxford: Blackwell.

——(1992) *Segregation Statistics: English LEAs*, London: CSIE.

Thomas, G. (1992) *Effective Classroom Teamwork*, London: Routledge.

——(1995) 'Special needs at risk?', *Support for Learning* 10, 3, 104–12.

Thomas, G. and Feiler, A. (eds) (1988) *Planning for Special Needs: A Whole School Approach*, Oxford: Blackwell.

Thomas, G., Walker, D. and Webb, J. (1998) *The Making of the Inclusive School*, London: Routledge.

Tizard, B., Blatchford, P., Burke, J., Farquhar, C. and Plewis, I. (1988) *Young Children at School in the Inner City*, London: Lawrence Erlbaum.

Tizard, B. and Hughes, M. (1984) *Young Children Learning*, London: Fontana.

Tizard, J., Schofield, W. N. and Hewison, J. (1982) 'Collaboration between teachers and parents in assisting children's reading', *British Journal of Educational Psychology* 52, 1–15.

Tomlinson Committee (1996) *Inclusive Learning: Report of the Learning Difficulties and/or Disabilities Committee*, London: FEFC.

Tomlinson, S. (1981) 'The social construction of the ESN(M) child', in L. Barton and S. Tomlinson (eds) *Special Education: Policies, Practices and Social Issues*, London: Harper & Row.

——(1982) *A Sociology of Special Education*, London: Routledge & Kegan Paul.

Topping, K. (1983) *Educational Systems for Disruptive Adolescents*, London: Croom Helm.

——(1986) *Parents as Educators: Training Parents to Teach Their Children*, London: Croom Helm.

——(1988) *The Peer Tutoring Handbook*, London: Croom Helm.

Topping, K. and Wolfendale, S. (eds) (1985) *Parental Involvement in Children's Reading*, London: Croom Helm.

Trier, S. (1997) 'Promoting the effective practice of partnership', in S. Wolfendale (ed.) *Working with Parents of SEN Children after the Code of Practice*, London: David Fulton.

TTA (1998) *National Standards for Special Educational Needs Coordinators*, London: TTA.

Tyler, R. W. (1949) *Basic Principles of Curriculum and Instruction*, Chicago: Chicago University Press.

Vaughan, M. (1989) 'Parents, children and the legal framework', in C. Roaf and H. Bines (eds) *Needs, Rights and Opportunities: Developing Approaches to Special Education*, Lewes: Falmer Press.

Vincent, C., Evans, J., Lunt, I. and Young, P. (1995) 'Policy and practice: the changing nature of special educational provision', *British Journal of Special Education* 22, 1, 4–11.

Watson, J. (1996) *Reflection through Interaction*, London: Falmer Press.

Webster, A. and Wood, D. J. (1989) *Children with Hearing Difficulties*, London: Cassell.

Wedell, K. (1995) 'Making inclusive education ordinary: a national perspective', *British Journal of Special Education* 22, 3, 100–4.

Wells, G. (1983) 'Talking with children: the complementary roles of parents and teachers', in M. Donaldson, R. Grieve and C. Pratt (eds) *Early Childhood Development and Education*, Oxford: Blackwell.

Welton, J. (1989) 'Incrementalism to catastrophe theory: policy for children with special educational needs', in C. Roaf and H. Bines (eds) *Needs, Rights and Opportunities: Developing Approaches to Special Education*, Lewes: Falmer Press.

Westwood, P. (1997) *Commonsense Methods for Children with Special Needs*, 3rd edn, London: Routledge.

Wheldall, K. and Merrett, F. (1984) *Positive Teaching: The Behavioural Approach*, London: Allen & Unwin.

White, M. (1997) 'A review of the influence and effects of Portage', in S. Wolfendale (ed.) *Working with Parents of SEN Children after the Code of Practice*, London: David Fulton.

White, M. and Cameron, S. (1987) *The Portage Early Education Programme*, Windsor: NFER-Nelson.

Williams, H. and Maloney, S. (1998) 'Well-meant, but failing on almost all counts: the case against statementing', *British Journal of Special Education* 25, 1, 16–21.

Wing, L. (1996) *The Autistic Spectrum: A Guide for Parents and Profes sionals*, London: Constable.

Wolfendale, S. (1987) *Primary Schools and Special Needs: Policy, Planning and Provision*, London: Cassell.

——(1988) *The Parental Contribution to Assessment*, Stratford-upon-Avon: NCSE

——(ed.) (1997) *Working with Parents of SEN Children after the Code of Practice*, London: David Fulton.

Wolfendale S. and Topping K. (eds) (1995) *Family Involvement in Literacy*, London: Cassell.

Index